# Aim Higher!

# Aim Higher!

*Spiritual and Marian reflections
of Saint Maximilian Kolbe*

A translation from the Polish
by Fr. Dominic Wisz, OFM CONV.

ISBN: 0-913382-59-0
MP 105-42

Third printing 2013

© 2007, Marytown Press,
1600 W. Park Ave., Libertyville, IL  60048.
847-367-7800.
www.marytown.com

# TABLE OF CONTENTS

## Part 3 Religious Life

Chapter

**Part 4  Thoughts .................................121**

**Part 5  Act of Consecration and Explanation**

**"Patron of our difficult century"**
—Pope John Paul II

S t. Maximilian Kolbe, OFM CONV., was born in Poland in 1894. As a seminarian in Rome he witnessed a well-organized Freemasons demonstration against the Catholic Church beneath the very windows of the Vatican. This event inspired him to found the Militia Immaculatae (MI) evangelization movement in October 1917.

Kolbe's method of outreach was to encourage each and every individuals to make a total consecration of himself to the Immaculate Virgin Mary. This act of abandonment would result in personal sanctification, the conversion of Church opponents and ultimately the establishment of the universal reign of the Sacred Heart of Jesus Christ.

After being ordained a priest, Father Maximilian began forming MI prayer groups and publishing a magazine, Knight of the Immaculata. The publishing ministry grew so rapidly that in 1927 he built an evangelization center near Warsaw called Niepokalanow—City of the Immaculata. By the time of the Nazi invasion of Poland in 1939, the City contained 650 friars and was the largest Catholic religious house in the world.

Kolbe utilized the most modern printing and administrative techniques available, enabling he and his friars to publish a daily newspaper and a number of periodicals. The Knight reached a circulation of over 1 million. Niepokalanow became the largest Catholic publishing house in Poland, perhaps in the world.

In his zeal to "win the world for the Immaculata," Kolbe in 1930 established a missionary center in Japan and had plans for centers in India and China. He built an airstrip to better distribute his newspapers, had his own radio station, and drew up plans for evangelizing through television and films.

While the Gestapo was thundering toward

Niepokalanow to whisk him away to the death camp, Kolbe hurried to complete his essay on Mary's self-title at Lourdes, France, "I am the Immaculate Conception." His keen insights further developed the Church's centuries-old understanding that the Blessed Virgin is the Mediatrix, or "gateway" of all the graces that flow to mankind from the Trinity. Pope Paul VI called Kolbe "clairvoyant" in his anticipation of the Marian theology of the Second Vatican Council. Pope John Paul II proclaimed him "Apostle of a new Marian era."

Father Maximilian was imprisoned in the Nazi concentration camp of Auschwitz in 1941, where he was singled out for special brutalities as a Catholic priest. In a supreme act of love, he defended the right to life of a prisoner who had been condemned to a starvation bunker by offering to take his place. Two weeks later, on August 14, 1941, Kolbe's impatient captors ended his life by a fatal injection. John Paul II canonized him a saint and "martyr of charity" in 1982.

Truly a saint of our difficult century, St. Maximilian Kolbe is the patron of journalists, prisoners, the prolife movement and, because of his manner of death, the chemically addicted.

*I command all my brothers, who are living now and who will live in the future, always to praise the Mother of God, and with every means to honor her everywhere as well as they are able, and have recourse to her with the greatest respect and surrender.*

—St. Francis of Assisi

*Our purpose is to win the world for the Immaculata.*

—St. Maximilian Kolbe

# Preface

There are moments in life when our long cherished ideals begin to lose color in our own eyes and die. But these are only passing moments. On the whole, when one takes an ideal seriously, he lives according to it and for it throughout his life. Having an ideal in life keeps us always young in spirit. It inspires daily progress towards divine goals, and constantly renews our strength. Like an eagle that uses his great wings to rise high into the blue sky, so a man with a spiritual ideal rises in thought high above the level of transient things, penetrating realities beyond the reach of ordinary eyes.

In 1928, coming in contact with Fr. Maximilian Kolbe for the first time, I was so struck by his supernatural charm that I had to restrain myself from crying out, "1 have never seen such a man before in all my life." And for us here at Niepokalanow also, the memory of St. Maximilian is cherished. And why? Because love of the Immaculata completely filled him and led him to point her and her mission out to us as the ideal for whom it is worthwhile to work, suffer and die.

But to keep the fire of an ideal alive, so that it becomes a source of action in practical life, it must be fed from day to day.

We have chosen sentences—sparks, as it were, from the fire of St. Maximilian's writings. Would that they bring forth in us each time we read them new and unshakable convictions regarding the mission of the MI that will inflame us to action!

NIEPOKALANOW, POLAND,
FEAST OF MARY,
MEDIATRIX OF ALL GRACES, 1944

## Preface to Revised Edition

This collection of excerpts, originally in Polish, are from the writings and conferences of St. Maximilian Kolbe. They were put together in the late 1940s, within seven years of the heroic death of the saint and decades before he was canonized. The Conventual Franciscan Friars of Marytown, his American "City of the Immaculata," published the excerpts to inspire the friars to better live their total consecration to Mary and thus be more faithful to their Franciscan vocation. These "sparks" from the original Kolbe's writings reach both the heart and the mind and were the first extensive translation of the saint's work from the Polish into English. The translator, Fr. Dominic Wisz, OFM CON., had been recently assigned to Marytown to take the place of the founder of Marytown, Fr. Dominic Szymanski, OFM CONV., who died in May of 1951.

The first English booklet, originally titled *My Ideal*, could not be circulated outside of Marytown, as the writings of Kolbe were under investigation since his cause for beatification had already been introduced. In those early days of Marytown the booklet was frequently found in the brother's places in chapel, along with *True Devotion to Mary*, by St. Louis de Montfort. It was this little booklet that I received as a candidate to the Marytown community in the summer of 1951 that convinced me that Kolbe's ideals had all that I was looking for in my quest of giving myself totally to God through Mary.

It wasn't a life-long search, for I was a late-comer in my devotion to Mary After one false start in regard to religious life, 1 made my act of total consecration according to St. Louis de Montfort's consecration on the feast of Mary's Assumption, August 15,1950, at the National Shrine of the Immaculate Conception.

I told her at that time I had evidently made a wrong choice in regard to my vocation, so I asked her to put me where she wanted me, not necessarily where I thought I should be. Less than three months later I found myself at Marytown, which was then located in Kenosha, Wisconsin.

At the time, the fledgling community didn't have much direction as its founder was dying of cancer and Fr. Cyril Kita, OFM CONV., the Father Provincial at the time, could not give the new friary the attention it needed. I wasn't exactly sure this community was for me. Fr. Dominic Szymanski, OFM CONV., saw the disappointment and counseled me. He told me that since I was at Marytown, evidently "She had arranged my being here." Who was I to contradict this holy man? Besides, I was reminded of my promise to our Lady of doing her will rather than my own. For the time being she evidently wanted me at Marytown.

I have to admit that the fact that Marytown was a Franciscan community did not influence me much in my decision of coming to Marytown, though my mother, brother and myself were Secular Franciscans in San Francisco, and I had two aunts who were Poor CIares. At the time I did not understand the close relationship between St. Francis, the Franciscan Order and our Lady.

That all changed when I found out that St. Maximilian, the latest in a long line of saints including the very founder of the Franciscan Order, had an outstanding devotion to Mary Immaculate. I discovered this fact, and more, in reading this booklet of "sparks that inflame" (as the first preface reads). I found my vocation in the Franciscans, a religious order second to none in its long tradition of devotion to Mary I found, much to my joy, a modern day saint who in his life and writings not only carried on that tradition but applied it heroically in his life, urging his followers to do the same.

Though our printery set up the type on the original *Aim Higher*, it was picked up by our friars in Africa, who for a long time were the only suppliers. I personally have circulated hundreds of these books. I owe much to our Lady in introducing me to *Aim Higher*. In this centennial year of the birth of St. Maximilian, what an opportune and providential occasion we have in acquainting more people with this treasure of great value, so vital in any true renewal. I pray that many, many other souls will be introduced and inspired by these sparks that inflame, and so make St. Maximilian's form of total consecration to Mary a central and vital part of their spiritual life.

BRO. FRANCIS MARY KALVELAGE, OFM CONV.
MARYTOWN, LIBERTYVILLE, ILLINOIS
March 1994

# Introduction

When you are preparing to read about the Immaculata do not forget that you are entering into contact with a living being—one who loves you, who is pure and without the least stain.

Remember, the words you read are not capable of expressing who she is because they are human words originally intended to express earthly ideas. But the Immaculata is a totally godlike being existing on an infinitely higher plane than all that surrounds you. She will be revealing herself to you through the sentences you read and will suggest thoughts, convictions, affections which have probably not even entered the author's mind. Finally, note that the purer your conscience is, and the more you cleanse it with penance, so much more will your idea of her approximate the truth.

Sincerely acknowledge this also, that without her aid you will not yourself be able in any measure to begin understanding her, and consequently, love her. She herself must enlighten you more and more and draw your heart with love towards herself. Therefore remember that the whole fruit of reading depends on prayer which is directed to her.

Do not begin to read before you have prayed to her. Do not try to read much, but interrupt your reading by lifting up your heart to her, especially when various affections arise in your heart. And when you finish your reading, confide to her the task of bringing forth in you an ever more bountiful harvest. Read not out of curiosity, but rather read a little well.

We should put into practice what we have read. It is sufficient to dedicate five minutes daily to this reading, but be resolute, and do not omit these five minutes any day. This will be an assurance of advancement in perfection. It will likewise be a healthful nourishment for our souls, because it will serve to give us wings in our flight to the summits of our desired holiness, and a closer union with the Immaculata.

Fr. Maximilian Maria Kolbe

# PART I
# THE IMMACULATA

# CHAPTER I

# Who is the Immaculata?

1. Who are you, my Lady? Who are you, Immaculata?

I cannot fathom what it is to be a creature of God. To understand what it means to be his adopted child is beyond my power. But you, O Immaculata, who are you? You are not only a creature, not just an adopted child, but the Mother of God—and not merely a foster Mother, but the real Mother of God. And this is not merely a supposition, a probability, but a certainty, an absolute certainty, a dogma of faith.

2. Who are you, O Immaculate Conception?

You are not God, because he has no beginning; not an angel created directly from nothing; not Adam, formed from the clay of the earth; not Eve, taken from Adam. Nor are you the Word Incarnate, who existed from all ages and is conceived rather than a conception. The children of Eve did not exist before conception, hence they can all the

3

more justly be called conceptions, and yet you are different from them all because they are conceptions stained by original sin. But you are alone the *Immaculate* Conception.

3. Immaculata: the summit of perfection of a creature, Mother of God, the most godlike of creatures.

The purpose of the creature, the purpose of man, is the progressive growth in likeness to the Creator, a constantly more perfect godliness. "God becomes man so that man might become God," says St. Augustine.

We imitate good, virtuous, holy people, but none of these is without imperfection. Only she, immaculate from the first moment of her existence, knows no fault, not the least. It is she whom one should imitate and come close to. We should become hers, become *her*. Behold the peak of perfection in man.

4. We call her Mother, but an earthly mother is not free from weakness. For that reason the constitutions of men make mention of the laws of children towards parents. Whereas this is a mother without stain, immaculate, and therefore any reservation on the part of the child would cause her unspeakable displeasure and wrong, for it would contain the supposition that even a shadow of stain

is not impossible in her. Quite the contrary, the child dedicated to her desires that she use him and wear him out; he desires to be consumed for her.

We name her *Lady*, but this title places us at a distance from her maternal heart. We call her *Queen*, but here we must add that she is the Queen of hearts, the Queen of love. Her law is love, and her power is motherly love. These and similar explanations, although they are brought forward without end, will not even tell a part of what the soul feels when it is consumed by love of her. It experiences in itself that the Immaculata belongs to it more and more under every aspect, and yet realizes that these are but the beginnings of knowing and loving her.

You will draw more knowledge about her and will be more inflamed with her love directly from her heart than from all human words put together.

5. The Immaculata.

Human words do not have the power to relate who she is—the real Mother of God. In reality, she is only a creature, but she is such a sublime being made by God that one would have to grasp what God is, in order to understand who the Mother of God is.

She is the real Mother of God. That is a dogma of faith. She is not a mother in name only. A mother is not the parent of only a part of her child, neither is the father the parent of a part, but both the father and mother are parents of the whole child. And so the Blessed Mother is rightly the Mother of the whole Jesus, the God-man, and therefore the Mother of God. Although the dignity of her maternity constitutes the principle reason for all her privileges, the first grace she received from God was her Immaculate Conception: freedom from every stain, even of original sin from the first moment of her existence.

This privilege must be dear to her, since she says of herself at Lourdes, "I am the Immaculate Conception." She does not say, "I am immaculately conceived," but "the Immaculate Conception." Hence it follows that she is immaculateness itself. She is truly Conception, for her existence began in time, but "Immaculate Conception."

6. The Immaculata at Lourdes does not call herself immaculately conceived, but, as St. Bernadette herself relates, "The Lady was standing above the wild rose bush in a position very similar to that shown on the Miraculous Medal. At my third request her face took on a serious expression, and at the same time an expression of deep humility. . . . Joining her palms as if for prayer, she raised them to the height of her breast. . . . She looked up to

heaven . . . then slowly opening her hands and bending down towards me, she said to me in a voice in which one could sense a slight trembling, 'I am the Immaculate Conception.'"

7. This title is proper to no one else but her. God, while revealing his name to Moses, said, "I am who am," because God is from all ages, forever and always. His essence is existence without limits, both in duration and from any other aspect. Everything else besides God is not existence, but has existence, having received it. Hence even the Immaculata began to exist in time.

8. "Immaculate Conception" does not mean, as some think, that the most Holy Virgin did not have a father on earth. She came forth as other children of this earth, having been born of a family and having a real father and mother.

She is called Conception. Therefore, she is not God, who has no beginning; neither an angel created directly by God; nor like the first parents who did not begin their existence by conception.

She is even called Conception not in the same way as Jesus, who, though conceived, nevertheless as God exists from eternity. But she is the *Immaculate* Conception. By this she differs from all other children of Adam. Thus the name Immaculate Conception is appropriate to her and to her alone.

9. Our Immaculate Mother and God's.

Where then is her place, and at the same time ours—we who are her property, her possession, hers? She penetrates our soul and sovereignly directs its faculties. We are truly hers. Therefore always, everywhere we are with her. But what are we to think of ourselves! Let us disappear in her. Let her alone remain and we in her, a part of her. Is it permitted to miserable creatures like us to talk such nonsense? And yet it is the truth, an actuality. When will every soul on the face of the whole earth, even until the end of the world, belong in such a manner to her? MI. MI. MI.

10. The Mother of God did not tell Bernadette at Lourdes, "I am immaculately conceived," but "I am the Immaculate Conception."

11. This truth that the Mother of God did not contract any stain of original sin from the first moment of her existence, was generally believed by all the faithful from the beginning of the Church and expressed in the sentiment that the Blessed Virgin was most pure, purer than the angels, without the least sin, and so on.

12. Our Father in heaven is the first beginning and final end of everything. The human tongue

and mind of man, in borrowing notions from his surroundings, falter when trying to think and speak about God. Imperfect is our notion of God. We know from divine revelation that from all ages and forever the Father brings forth the Son, and the Spirit proceeds from the Father and the Son. This life of the Holy Trinity is imitated in numberless and diverse images of the creatures coming from the hands of the Triune God, according as they more or less resemble him. The general principle that each effect is similar to the cause has its full application here and all the more so, since God creates from nothing. Therefore whatever is in creation is his handiwork.

From the Father through the Son and Spirit descends each act of the love of God, creating, sustaining in existence, giving life and its development both in the order of nature as well as in the order of grace. In such a manner does God bestow his love on countless finite images. And by no other way does the return of the reaction of the creature's love ascend to the Father except through the Spirit and the Son. This does not always happen consciously, but always really. No one else but the same God is the author of the act of love in creatures. But the act does not take place without the creature's free will and consent.

The height of a creature's love returning to God is the Immaculata—a being without stain of sin, wholly beautiful, wholly belonging to God. Not even for a moment did her will bend away from the will of God.

13. The Immaculata is someone so sublime, so close to the most Holy Trinity that one of the Holy Fathers did not hesitate to call her *complementum Sanctissimae Trinitatis,* i.e., complement of the most Holy Trinity. No wonder, then, the human, finite mind loses itself when it attempts to fathom her mystery, and the presumptuous head grows more stupid. Let everyone at Marytown know about these things.

14. The most important work entrusted to humanity, that is, the bearing and upbringing of Jesus, God entrusted to the most Blessed Mother. Therefore, can there be any comparison of the most Blessed Mother with other saints? There is none.

15. From the divine motherhood flow all the graces bestowed upon the Holy Virgin Mary. The first of these is the Immaculate Conception. This privilege must be very dear to her since she said at Lourdes, "I am the Immaculate Conception." By this name so dear to her heart we wish to call her.

16. In order to understand more accurately who the Immaculata is, it is absolutely necessary to ad-

mit one's total nothingness, to bring oneself to humble prayer in order to gain the grace of knowing her, and to endeavor personally to experience her goodness and power.

17. Why do we love the Immaculata and wholly dedicate ourselves to her?

Not for what she is in herself, but because she is godlike.

18. The loftiest of creatures is man; of men, in turn, the Immaculata is the most perfect, without the least sin, immaculate.

19. The Immaculata is the personification of the mercy of God. For that reason he who rises against her pushes from himself that mercy, and draws down upon himself the justice of God.

20. The little infant that draws away from his mother and refuses his mother's breast will perish from hunger. In the same way one who draws away from the Blessed Mother will perish from spiritual hunger.

21. Our commandress, the Immaculata, refuge of sinners, is also the vanquisher of the hellish serpent.

22. All that is created is finite and develops more and more with time, but she, the Immaculata, touches upon infinity.

23. If we render honor to the mother of a famous

man, a benefactor of humanity, with what honor ought we give the Mother of the Son of God!

24. If the mother of a ruler is influential with her son, how influential must be the Mother of the God-man!

25. Every grace is a new proof of the power and the goodness of the Immaculata. Therefore she is what we consider her.

26. There is nothing a man cannot bear through the Immaculata.

27. Mary always was to us a most tender Mother, and is now, and always will be, in life and in death and in eternity. Let us recall this truth to ourselves often in external difficulties, but especially in those more grievous internal ones.


## CHAPTER 2

# Mediatrix of All Graces

1. An absolute and irrefutable sentiment in the Catholic Church, although it is not yet declared a dogma, is that the Mother of God is the Mediatrix of All Graces. During the first centuries of Christianity this truth was already known.

The work of the *Militia Immaculatae* and of the

*Knight (Rycerz)* depends precisely upon the truth that the Immaculata is the Mediatrix of All Graces. If it were not so, our whole activity of the MI would be illogical.

2. The Holy Spirit does not act except through the Immaculata, his spouse. Hence she is the Mediatrix of all the graces of the Holy Spirit.

3. It irks me at times to read the overcareful emphasis that *after Jesus* the Mother of God is our entire hope. Certainly it is possible to interpret this phrase correctly. But this excessive carefulness in order to pay respect to Jesus without omitting this phrase seems to my mind to bring discredit to him. Let us imagine: A rotary press arrives just when the platen presses were not sufficient, and we can justly say that in order to publish the *Knight* on schedule our whole hope rested upon the rotary. If, nevertheless, someone would immediately add "after the factory" (which built the press), he would thus give the impression that the machine could break down and would have to be returned to the factory. In other words the factory did not build the press very durably. This would scarcely be a compliment to the factory.

4. The Immaculata is the Mediatrix of Graces. She is overflowing with grace, and we receive from that superabundance of grace.

5. If we were to look into the interior of our soul, we would see how much activity of the Immaculata there is and has been in our souls from the dawn of our lives to the present moment, and how much assurance of her benefits for the future. These are for the most part mysteries of each individual soul. It is enough to mention that every grace received each day, hour, and moment of our life is her grace, flowing from her motherly heart that loves us.

6. In her womb the soul must be regenerated according to the form of Jesus Christ. She must nourish the soul with the milk of her grace, caress and rear us in the manner in which she nourished and brought up Jesus. The soul must learn to know and to love Jesus at her knees. Let us draw love for him from her heart. Yes, love him with her heart, and through love become like him.

7. The end of every man is to be godlike through Jesus, who is the Mediator with the Father, and of Jesus through the Mediatrix of All Graces, the Immaculata.

8. It is incredible that anyone should approach Jesus without Mary. Why? For, omitting the very fact that she brought forth Jesus and raised him for us, the approach to Jesus is without doubt a grace in itself. But all graces come to us through her in the way that Jesus himself came. Is it then

permitted to converse directly with Jesus, if I do not think of Mary? It is not a question of feeling or thinking, but of the fact itself that it is so, even though the thought of her intercession would never cross your mind. If you really love Jesus, then above all you desire to do his will in all things, and receive graces in the way that he ordained. When you have such a disposition you can and ought freely turn to the Sacred Heart of Jesus being confident that you will obtain everything. If someone however were to tell himself, "I do not need any medication, I do not need the Blessed Mother, I myself am able to praise and honor the most Sacred Heart of God and ask for what I need"—would Jesus not cast him justly aside for such insufferable pride?

9. Through the Immaculata we can become great saints, and what is more, in an easy way.

10. The Immaculata as the Mediatrix of All Graces, not only can and desires to give the grace of conversion and sanctity at certain times and places, but she wants to regenerate all souls, and moreover, our [Franciscan] Order.

11. What does conversion and sanctification through the Immaculata mean? It means that the grace needed for conversion and sanctification comes through the Immaculata.

12. "I am able to do all things in him who strengthens me" through the Immaculata. And why through the Immaculata?

God in his infinite goodness, not wishing to punish us for our failings, pledged himself by the Blessed Mother. The Holy Fathers say that God divided his kingdom into two parts: he left justice for himself, and to his Blessed Mother he gave mercy. Thus we have the right to add "through the Immaculata."

Whatever happens for the cause of conversion and sanctification is a work of the grace of God. But the Mediatrix of that grace is the Mother of God. As Jesus is sole Mediator with God the Father, so the only Mediatrix with Jesus is the Mother of God. Therefore, conversion and sanctification come through her.

13. Our gifts become immaculate in the Immaculata. In Jesus Christ they become divine, infinite, worthy of the majesty of God the Father.

Jesus is the only Mediator to the Father, the Immaculata, the only Mediatrix to Jesus.

14. What Mary gives to Jesus is unsoiled, and Jesus then renders it to God the Father in an infinite way. The honor, then, which we give to Jesus through Mary is unsoiled and infinite.

15. Our life on this earth is to be the prolonga-

tion of the life of Jesus through Mary.

16. With the help of the Immaculata we are capable of everything.

17. The nearer we come to the Immaculata, the more we become holy. The Mother of God is the Mediatrix of All Graces, and holiness is the work of the grace of God. The devil knows that the nearer we are to the Immaculata, the more graces we receive from her hands. That is why he tries at all costs to draw the soul away from the Blessed Mother, even under the guise of devotion to Jesus. He knows that God established such a way through the Immaculata, and he likewise knows that when the soul departs from this way, it will not receive as many graces. Therefore whether we feel aversion, whether we are in darkness or in light, let us always advance by way of the Immaculata. It is a very important matter that our life be lived *through her, with her and in her.*

18. The Immaculata is the ladder upon which we climb to the Sacred Heart of Jesus. Whoever removes this ladder will not reach the top and will crash to the ground. We strongly believe that she leads us to Jesus. Let whoever teaches otherwise be anathema! Let him be anathema!

19. If we wish to love Jesus with the heart of the Immaculata, receive him with her heart, praise him

17

with her acts, make reparation and at the same time give thanks through her. Even if we were not to feel and understand this way, nevertheless it is so. Then with her heart, with her acts we praise Jesus, or actually, it is she who loves and praises Jesus through us. We are then her instruments.

## CHAPTER 3

# The Will of the Immaculata

1. Christian perfection consists in the union of our will with the will of God. The will of the Immaculata is closely united with the will of God, so that it seems as if there were but one will. Since we are speaking of doing the will of God, we can at the same time boldly say that we are doing the will of the Immaculata. By this we do not detract from the glory of God, but rather we add to it. When we so act, we make manifest the perfection of Mary as the most perfect creature of God and the complete union of her will with the will of God. Do not be afraid, dear children, to say, "It is the will of the Immaculata," because it is the same as the will of God.

2. There is no doubt that the will of the

Immaculata is wholly united to the will of God. The problem is only to unite our will with her will so that through her we might be united with God.

3. Whoever would say that he does not wish to serve the Mother of God is obedient to the devil, for it is the will of God that we do not exclude the Mother of God.

4. We accomplish the most for the happiness of souls when we perfectly perform the will of the Immaculata, our commandress.

5. Whatever does not depend on our will is surely the will of the Immaculata. Whatever should come even from evil and perverse people is certainly the will of God, certainly permitted by God, and therefore the will of the Immaculata.

6. If we say, "It is the will of the Immaculata," besides the fact that we acknowledge the will of God by this phrase, we also honor the Blessed Mother, inasmuch as we acknowledge that her will is so fused with the will of God that it constitutes one intimate union. In addition, we give more honor to God by recognizing his perfection in creating such a great, powerful, good and holy being as the Blessed Mother.

7. I would be altogether happy at the moment of death if all those at the City of the Immaculata would in all things recognize the *Immaculata*. When

this is brought about everything will be done; when it is absent, everything will fall apart.

## CHAPTER 4

# Our Ideal

1. Behold our ideal—the Immaculata.

To come close to her, to become like her, to permit her to reign over our hearts and our whole being, that she live and act in us and through us, that she love God with our hearts and we belong to her unreservedly—this is our ideal. To influence those who surround us in order that also the hearts of our neighbors might open, so that she might be Queen in the hearts of all men wherever they are in the world, without regard for the difference of race, nationality, language, even in the hearts of all who will live until the end of the world—this is our ideal.

That her life might grow deeper in us from day to day, from hour to hour, from moment to moment and without any limits—this is our ideal.

2. To give one's life for the Immaculata is the summit of love!

3. The ideal of Marytown is to *resemble the*

*Immaculata* as much as possible.

4. We think too little about the Immaculata. We read too little about her, too seldom do we approach her.

5. Whenever it is a question of the Immaculata, of her work, then it is never too much, never enough! But rather it is a question of doing more, becoming better, holier, more perfect!

6. Were Marytown to *cross out* the Immaculata as the ladder to perfection it would lose all. There must be a battle for the highest Ideal.

**CHAPTER 5**

# Confidence

1. When a storm strikes a ship out at sea, the ship does not stop, does not struggle, but peacefully sails onward. Similarly when the storm in our soul rages, we should not struggle, we should not lose our peace, but turn toward the Immaculata and then go forward with absolute confidence.

2. If the thought of your past life and sins oppresses you and you have no courage to look into the future beyond the grave, give yourself to the Immaculata wholeheartedly, without restriction.

Entrust her with the work of your whole salvation, your whole life, death and eternity. You will perceive what peace and happiness is, a foretaste of heaven, and you will sigh for heaven.

3. If we have a difficulty, let us hasten to the Immaculata.

4. Be confident that from *her* you will surely receive all that you need both for salvation and perseverance in the [Franciscan] Order and for sanctification. Storms will come, it is true, but he who sincerely loves the Immaculata will pass through these tempests, no matter how dangerous, entirely untouched and unsullied by sin.

5. Let us have no confidence in ourselves. At the same time *let us not place any bounds to our confidence in her.* In every difficulty and temptation let us have recourse to her, and we will assuredly not fall. Let us entrust to her every undertaking, and we will surely attain whatever she wants.

6. Nothing will happen, dear children, except whatever the Immaculata will permit. Let us hand over all our difficulties to her, and for the rest, be at peace.

7. It is our ideal to win the whole world for the Immaculata and through her hands the souls who are and who will be, all of them collectively and each of them individually.

When we say "through the hands of Mary," we should not understand this exteriorly, but as something interior. Whatever we do we give to her as her own. We give ourselves and our belongings to her as her property. She in turn gives it to Jesus as her own. These are very profound matters, and we learn them in humble prayer.

## CHAPTER 6

# Surrendering Ourselves to the Immaculata

1. The essence of surrender depends on the will. Insofar as the will places an act and has not retracted it, the surrender remains henceforth valid, even if we do not actually think about it. A carpenter, for example, makes a table to order. Does he necessarily have to continuously reflect that he is making that table to order, or that the table is for this or that customer? He could busy himself with the work and not think in any way about it, and yet he progresses toward his goal.

If then we place the act and do not retract it, all that which we have surrendered to the Immaculata

23

belongs to her, even though we do not think about it in the least.

2. Whoever has surrendered himself to the Immaculata in the spirit of the MI feels that he depends upon her in everything; he no longer belongs to himself, but truly to her, the Immaculata, the Mother of God, who is the true and gracious queen of heaven and earth.

3. We have surrendered all to the Immaculata. Hence whatever is ours is her property! Her plans are ours, her virtues, merits—all are ours. All depends on whether we will it. Extraordinary prayers or mortifications are not necessary. We have only to let her lead us on.

4. We are wholly, entirely and exclusively surrendered to the Immaculata with all our acts, and in her and through her wholly, entirely and exclusively given to Jesus, and in him and through him wholly, entirely and exclusively given to our Father in heaven.

5. The essence of the surrender to the Immaculata does not depend on a continual awareness of her but on the will. A soul wholly occupied with the proper fulfillment of its duty does not cease to belong to the Immaculata. Its thoughts, words, and actions do not cease to belong to the

Immaculata even though the soul does not think of it.

6. He alone will spend his life well who constantly turns to the Immaculata. In her alone is the pledge of our perseverance and sanctification.

7. First of all we must give ourselves for the Immaculata, so in us and through us she may operate in others. Let us draw near to her and imitate her virtues, that we might merit to behold her throughout eternity.

8. When there is opposition meet it; in spite of it draw more closely to the Immaculata, speak to her as a little child. Submit all to her will. Whether she wishes to give us sweets or feed us on aridity, do not mind. Be near her with your will, folded in her arms.

9. In order to persevere and advance in this surrender to the Immaculata, you must continually refresh your mind with these truths and your relationship to the Immaculata, either from a suitable book or from meditation or the like. For the most part, though, this will be dictated by the Immaculata herself during humble prayer.

10. You can make an agreement with the Immaculata. Every time you return from distraction to that activity that she desires and she, through holy obedience, either directly or by im-

plication has set down for you, so often will you renew the surrender of yourselves, your activity and all that is yours to the Immaculata without restriction.

11. What can happen to us, surrendered as we are to the Immaculata? The most anyone can do is to take our life. But then they will render us the greatest service, because we will be able to "take them" by the hand with both hands—or rather by the heart—so that they will take our places on earth. Only then will we be able to subdue the whole earth for the Immaculata.

12. We have surrendered ourselves to the Immaculata as instruments, hence she is to work through us. We know it takes a writer to use a pen. Although we say that something is written by a pen, yet the pen itself cannot write, but only the writer. We are to be pens in the hand of the Immaculata.

13. The more one belongs to the Immaculata, the greater is one's boldness and daring in drawing near to the wounds of the Savior, the Eucharist, to the Sacred Heart of Jesus and to God the Father. It does not hurt even if at times the thought of the Immaculata does not enter our mind, because the essence of union with her depends not on thought, memory or affection, but upon the will.

14. We must go the way of surrender to the Immaculata, and that most perfectly. Then we shall act most effectively because the Immaculata will act through us.

15. Our most important activity is to endeavor to live in such a way that daily, more and more, we become her property, hers completely.

16. Our acts, even the holiest, are not without stain. And if we want to offer them to Jesus chaste and immaculate, we must straightaway and singlemindedly wend our way to the Immaculata and give our acts to her as her own, so that as her property she offer them to her Son. Then they will be without stain, immaculate. Once having received infinite value through the divinity of Jesus, our acts will worthily honor God the Father.

17. In every Franciscan friary, even the most fervent, only two things are strictly obligatory: the Rule and the Constitutions. But at Marytown a third one is binding, the certificate of the MI. According to its most precise meaning it indicates a surrender of oneself without reserve to the Immaculata. And why? Because of offerings poured in for this purpose. It is because of these offerings that the *Knight*, the Marytowns in Poland and Japan arose, and wherever else the Immaculata desires them to arise until the Immaculata will

27

enter and become queen in every heart.

18. We are an instrument in the most loving hands of the Immaculata, and only in this manner can we attain our—the Militia's—ultimate goal: not only the greater glory of God but the greatest. Our whole endeavor must therefore be to allow ourselves to be led, so that we do nothing of ourselves, but whatever and however she wishes.

19. We have given ourselves without reserve to the Immaculata; hence we no longer have any right over our thoughts, our actions, our words. Let her alone rule us according to her pleasure. Let her graciously disregard our will. If we want to pull away from her immaculate hand in any circumstance, let her compel us even though we should protest and refuse and beg off. Let her pay attention to nothing, but compel us forcefully and thus press us yet more forcefully to her heart.

20. We are instruments of the Immaculata, but not by physical force, as a brush in the hand of an artist, but rather guided by intellect and will.

21. If only we would give over the leadership of ourselves to the Immaculata, she would do everything, even though a miracle were necessary. For even a miracle does not present any difficulty to her.

22. Whenever a person, who wholly and unreservedly surrenders himself to the Immaculata, visits Jesus in the Blessed Sacrament, he dedicates his whole visit more explicitly to the Immaculata even though by only one "Mary!" He knows that he affords Jesus the greatest pleasure, that thus she makes that visit in him and through him, and he in her and through her.

23. The Immaculata is good and, indeed so good that despite so many frailties she is not discouraged with us. Although she herself is immaculate, yet she does not recoil from using rusty tools to carry out her works of conversion and sanctification, or of supernaturally stimulating and developing souls.

24. Everyone should be desirous that the Immaculata unreservedly capture his heart to the fullest extent. Our surrender to the Immaculata must be necessarily without bounds, irrevocable, without restrictions, not only in this or that employment but in all of them, without limits, without any limits. On our part we must deepen this limitless dedication, because in the domain of our own ego no one can interfere. The more perfectly one places himself in the hands of the Immaculata the more perfectly will he be an instrument in her hands. And then on the grounds of Marytown she

will reign through us. *Everything depends on this limitless dedication to her.*

25. The nearer we draw to the Immaculata the happier will the whole Marytown be. If a soul does not reach the level of surrender to her, it will not enjoy happiness.

26. The more we belong to the Immaculata, the more perfectly will we understand and love Jesus, God the Father and the whole Blessed Trinity.

27. To dedicate oneself without reserve to the Immaculata means to always be ready to work wherever she might wish. Therefore we must be ready to leave for the missions, or to set out today for Moscow or Madrid on foot, if such were the will of the Immaculata.

If we object with only one "but," the dedication would not be without reserve. Nor must we understand our dedication in any other sense when it concerns our occupations in the friary.

28. Our interior life must be such that we are tools in the hands of the Immaculata, in other words to permit her to guide us in all things.

29. Both you and I are the property and possession of the Immaculata forever. May she herself exclusively and at her pleasure do with our person, our life, death and eternity whatever pleases her.

30. Let us imagine that we are a brush in the hand of an infinitely perfect artist. What must a brush do to make the painting turn out most beautiful? It must allow itself to be guided as perfectly as possible. The brush might still have pretensions to correct an earthly, finite, fallible artist. But when eternal wisdom, God, uses us as an instrument, then we shall act most fruitfully and most perfectly when we permit ourselves to be directed most perfectly and entirely.

By an act of consecration we have dedicated ourselves to the Immaculata as her total possession. Without doubt she is the most perfect instrument in the hands of God. We in turn should be instruments in her immaculate hands.

How soon and how completely will we defeat the evil in the whole world? When we allow ourselves to be guided by her most completely. This is our most important and our only business.

31. Let us remember that the essence of our dedication to the Immaculata and our perfection of dedication does not consist in a continual feeling or remembrance of it, but in our will. If then someone would not sense the sweetness of intimacy with her at all (although it is ordinarily otherwise), nor be continually mindful of her, nor think much of her for some reason or another, but if his will

sticks by her and does not retract its surrender, and still renews it according to its ability, then let him be at peace, because she reigns in his heart.

32. Every day let us all the more become the Immaculata's and in her and through her of Jesus, of God. Let us not serve God the Father *and* Jesus *and* the Immaculata, but God in Jesus and through him, and Jesus in the Immaculata and through the Immaculata. In other words, let us belong to the Immaculata directly, unreservedly and exclusively. Then with her, in her and through her we belong to Jesus. And with him, in him and through him we belong to God the Father.

### CHAPTER 7

## Love

1. The love of the Immaculata is the most perfect love with which a creature can love God. With her heart then let us strive to love the Heart of Jesus more and more. Let this be our greatest stimulus.

Let us try to win not only many, but all souls for the Immaculata, and unite them as closely as possible to the most sweet Heart of Jesus through her. But first subdue your own heart and then the hearts of others.

2. Every thought, action, suffering of the Immaculata were most perfect acts of love of God, love of Jesus.

It is necessary to tell all souls, both collectively and individually, those who are living now and who will live until the end of the world; it is necessary to tell them by example, by the spoken, written and printed word, by radio, painting, sculpture and so on. We must tell them what and how the Immaculata would think, speak and act in the concrete circumstances of daily living in the various states of life, so that the most perfect love, a love reaching even to that of the Immaculata towards the heart of God, would be enkindled all over the earth.

3. The essence of the love of God consists exclusively in fulfilling the will of God at every moment. The more difficult that fulfillment, the more horror and aversion it entails, the greater will be the manifestation of love. But even these difficulties do not belong to the essence of love. And, in fact, there can be love without them. They serve only to display that love.

4. Let us emulate one another when it concerns the Immaculata. May every increase of love towards her in one person result in a greater strengthening of love in others. Our hearts are so small, so

weak. We will never render her the love that she deserves, the love with which she loves us.

5. Let us all endeavor to deepen our love more and more towards the Immaculata, and always to have recourse to her as children towards their mother.

6. One act of perfect love regenerates the soul. Let us make use of this means often. It really is not so difficult, because the essence of this act is sacrificial love: to try to give pleasure to the Immaculata at one's own expense without regard to reward or punishment.

7. The essence of the love of God does not lie in affections or in sweet words, but solely in the will. If the soul perseveres decisively with its will fixed on holiness and love of God, although it does not experience the least feeling in its heart, let it be wholly convinced that it continually tends with rapid pace forward and ever pushes upward.

8. Love, which is a "bond of perfection," nourishes and satisfies itself solely by suffering, sacrifice and the cross.

9. We will show the greatest love towards the Immaculata when we share our love for her with others.

10. How can we prove the Immaculata loves us?

If we love her, then she loves us incomparably more.

11. What is unrestricted love of the Immaculata?

The Immaculata is so joined with God by love that she rises not only above all the saints, but also above the angels and archangels, the Cherubim and Seraphim. Therefore, unrestricted love of the Immaculata raises us up even to her and unites us in a love above that of all the angels and saints.

She is the nearest to God, and we the nearest to her, and hence through her the nearest to God himself. God has given us that white ladder and desires that we climb up upon it to reach him. Or rather she, holding us close to her maternal breast, brings us up to God.

But these are only pictures, resemblances, analogies. Reality is incomparably more beautiful, more sublime, divine.

## CHAPTER 8

# The Feast of the Immaculate Conception

1. Let us take care to prepare as best we can for the special feast of the Knights of the Immaculata on December 8, to rejuvenate ourselves in the Immaculata, to make reparation for the past year, which was not as it should have been.

2. Let each one ask himself whether he has worked during the year as much as he was able for the Immaculata, for salvation and sanctification of his own soul and the souls of his neighbors, and whether his conscience reproaches him for laziness, negligence, insufficient zeal and perhaps a lack of sacrifice.

Let us look into ourselves. Let December 8 be a day of regeneration for our souls, a renewal of zeal for furthering the heavenly and earthly kingdom of the most loving queen.

3. Would that on the occasion of the feast of the Immaculate Conception we become increasingly and more quickly her own, her property, her possession, her slaves and so on—in a word hers; hers

in the strictest acceptation of the word; most perfectly hers in life, death and eternity!

If only we would draw others to such an observance of this feast day, and that as soon as possible.

PART TWO

# THE MILITIA IMMACULATAE
# AND MARYTOWN

# CHAPTER I

# The Essence and Purpose of the MI

1. The essence of the MI consists in its belonging to the Immaculata unconditionally, irrevocably, without restriction, and this under every aspect.

2. The MI began and developed through holy obedience. And it could not be otherwise, for its essence is to be *of the Immaculata*, the Immaculata's servant and child and slave and thing and property and so on; in brief, to be hers under every aspect. Make yourself disappear and become as if her. The most essential element in such a transformation is the adjustment, the fusion, the union of our will with hers.

3. The ultimate purpose of man is the purpose toward which he tends, and for which he uses the means of attaining it.

The love of God through and in the Immaculata is our purpose, and our life is our means. Consequently we should use up our life for that purpose.

4. To win as many souls as possible for the Immaculata is our life, our breath, our every heart beat. Thus we dedicate ourselves to the Immaculata more and more, unconditionally and irrevocably, and to engraft this dedication in the heart of everyone in the whole world, so that she might be able to rule at will in our hearts and in the hearts of everyone in the world. In other words we must bring about the accomplishment of the purpose of the MI in the whole world, as swiftly as possible, and then remain watchful so that no one remove the banner of the Immaculata from any heart.

What an enormous work!

And then death, after a life so laborious, long-suffering and utterly used up for the Immaculata!

5. To bend the proud neck of the world to the feet of the Immaculata is the purpose of the MI: to win the whole world and every soul in particular for her as soon as possible, as soon as possible, as soon as possible. Then the kingship of the Sacred Heart of Jesus will reign through her upon the earth.

It is absolutely necessary to gain the whole world for her, so that the reign of sin will cease.

6. What do we wish to say by the words, "strive for the conversion and sanctification of souls

through the Immaculata?" What do we stress by these words?

We wish to emphasize that the shortest, surest way to conversion and sanctification is the Immaculata. We ourselves wish to advance on this road and teach it to others.

7. Through the Immaculata we will attain the ultimate purpose of the MI, that is, the greatest possible glory of God.

8. There are two sentences placed at the beginning of the charter of the MI: "She will crush thy head" and "Thou alone hast destroyed all heresies in the whole world." In these two concepts is embodied the purpose of the *Militia Immaculatae*. And that is why the members of the MI dedicate themselves to the Immaculata unreservedly as tools in her hand, so that through the members she will deign to accomplish what was spoken of her in these sentences.

9. The purpose of the *Militia Immaculatae* is to gain the whole world, all hearts and each one in particular for the Queen of both heaven and earth. It is our goal to give real happiness to those poor souls who seek happiness in the passing pleasures of this world.

## CHAPTER 2

# The Form and Purpose of the MI

1. That which constitutes the essence of every society, or that which unites the members in tending towards the end, is its form. In the MI the form is the entire and unrestricted dedication to the Immaculate Virgin Mary, so that she might deign to perform in and through us what has been written of her, "She will crush thy head" and "Thou alone has destroyed all heresies in the whole world."

2. The spirit is what vivifies and urges us on. The spirit of the MI will give life to its members, so that they may be Knights of the Immaculata more and more, and so that they may daily become more and more the property and possession of the Immaculata, and more zealously win for her the hearts of their neighbors. The more they are imbued with this spirit, the greater Knights of the Immaculata they will be.

3. It seems to me—maybe it is too utopian—that the normal state of affairs at Marytown should be that the future workers who are to conquer the world for the Immaculata form themselves at Marytown in its spirit, that is, by unrestricted dedi-

cation to the Immaculata according to the spirit of the MI certificate; but only those who do this, because others, not being obliged to this unrestricted dedication, would have a detracting influence.

## CHAPTER 3

# The Motto of the MI

The motto of the *Militia Immaculatae* is "To lead all men and every individual through Mary to the most Sacred Heart of Jesus." In other words, the Immaculata must become the queen of each and every soul.

## CHAPTER 4

# Essence, Purpose and Character of Marytown

1. The purpose of Marytown is the fulfillment of the purpose of the MI.
2. First of all we must conquer our own souls

for the Immaculata, and through her for the Sacred Heart of Jesus.

The pen, the chisel, the brush in the hands of the master create beautiful masterpieces for the very reason that they are completely submissive and obedient to him. Similarly we must form our will and permit the Immaculata to do whatever she pleases with us. This is the most important bastion in our offensive which we must take.

Meanwhile we must conquer Marytown—conquer it by helping our fellow brothers in the work of winning their own souls. Above all let us help by our example, a good word, encouragement, support.

The more of our own pleasure that we sacrifice for this mutual aid, the greater will the result be, and the more will the Immaculata bless this offensive, and the more will our own souls benefit.

3. In Marytown the immediate end is the Immaculata. Marytown is named after her because everything in it, including ourselves, belongs to her.

4. Our ideal is to win the whole world: the souls, who are now and will be, collectively and individually, for the Immaculata and through her hands.

5. At times I fear Marytown would be considered as just one more friary that had become ca-

pable of supporting the minor seminary of the province, and not as a work *of the Immaculata*, built from the money given *for spreading the honor of the Immaculata*. For fear of committing an injustice it is not permitted to turn one penny to any other purpose, however noble. It is only *for the cause of the Immaculata*, since we are *not allowed* to use those offerings for any other purpose than for which they were given.

We are only the stewards of the offerings obtained from the MI members and from the readers of the *Knight*, who made offerings to the *Knight* in order to conquer the world for the Immaculata. These offerings are not to be used according to our will!

6. The most important task of Marytown is the sanctification of the brothers, our own sanctification. We must continuously remember this because this is very important: *self-sanctification*.

7. Does not Marytown have a special purpose which constitutes the reason for its existence, namely, to conquer the whole world for the Immaculata in the spirit of the MI? This is the realization of the purpose of the MI!

8. In case of dispersion in time of war, each one of us must be a "type" of Marytown, in order that our spirit be preserved from worldly influences.

Whereupon in these circumstances we will both sanctify ourselves more and draw others to the Immaculata.

9. The administration of the MI is, as it were, a chancery of the Immaculata. Therefore it is necessary to handle all matters as the Immaculata herself would handle them.

10. The purpose of Marytown will always be the conquering of the whole world for the Immaculata as soon as possible, and everything in it. Both workers and inanimate objects will function solely for that purpose. Otherwise there will be no reason for its existence, and slowly it will begin to approach dissolution.

11. The *essence* of Marytown is to belong to the Immaculata, as a whole and in every part, in every soul living there.

We have to take care that we become hers more and more, that the "City of the Immaculata" (Marytown) become more and more the city of the Immaculata.

12. The distinguishing character of Marytown lies in its *unreserved* surrender to the Immaculata to conquer the whole world for her. Hence everyone must be ready at any moment to go anywhere without hesitation, even to the ends of the earth and to a sure death. In a word, always and in ev-

erything: "unreservedly" for the Immaculata.

13. What if Marytown should fail?

If the Immaculata should wish that it fail, then we all would strive to aid her eminently. For indeed she is its owner and has absolute right at any moment if she so wishes to say, "It is enough." If, on the other hand, she does not will it, then there is no fear, even though all by their failings would be more of a hindrance than theretofore. It is enough if, "after waking up" and "opening our eyes," we would immediately and unreservedly give to her ourselves and all that we have done wrong. She is always able to turn all this to even greater good.

How comforting is this truth, how deep a peace it brings us! She is the manager. Let us allow her to direct us more and more perfectly.

14. What is the essence of our foundation? Why does Marytown exist? What distinguishes it from others? What does it emphasize in a special way?

We already have so many orders, so many monasteries, so many zealous souls, striving to convert and sanctify other souls. So much has already been done at various times in Poland and outside of Poland.

Why then Marytown? In what does it differ from others?

It differs by reason of this special character: "To strive for *the conversion and sanctification of souls under the protection and through the mediation of the Immaculata.*"

The difference is not "striving for the conversion and sanctification of souls," towards which everyone tends, but *"through the Immaculata,"* which is added at the end. These two words are our special characteristic.

We may not say that others should not work in the same manner. Everyone knows that the Mother of God is the Mediatrix of All Graces; hence they value their devotion to her. But the question here concerns a special characteristic, *through the Immaculata,* and this is the *essence of Marytown and the Militia.*

If we wished to go into detail and analyze these words, then we would say that we place a special stress on the word *Immaculata,* if only for the reason that she thus named herself. It is apparent that this is a deep matter and very dear to her.

15. Our purpose and the purpose of Marytown is to win the world for the Immaculata. For this end we live, work and suffer, and with the aid of the Immaculata will die for it.

16. Every action, even the smallest such as ordinary sweeping, is to be for the Immaculata, and

must measure up to our purpose, the ideal of the MI.

17. The purpose of Marytown is to accomplish the end pointed out in the certificate of the MI, to win all the souls who are and will be, collectively and individually, for the Immaculata, and through her for the most Sacred Heart of Jesus. This must be done as soon as possible, as soon as possible, as soon as possible.

18. The modes of functioning in the Church are as diverse as flowers in a meadow. Marytown takes care of the *affairs of the Immaculata exclusively*, which is the sole purpose of the MI, but then with as much vigor and as widely as possible.

19. If Marytown has for its end the affairs of the Immaculata, it cannot desire anything else. A lily cannot desire to be a rose.

*If Marytown crosses out the Immaculata as the ladder to perfection, it loses everything.* We must do battle for the highest ideal!

20. St. Paul says in his letter to the faithful, "But . . . even though an angel from heaven preach a gospel to you besides that which we have preached to you, let him be anathema!"

Similarly I repeat to you that if someone should arise among you who would not wish to honor the Blessed Mother, and that in a special manner,

51

who would loosen our close bond with the Immaculata and teach something other than what I teach you, let him be *anathema!*

21. The unreservedness of dedicating oneself to the Immaculata is our necessary aim, for otherwise our whole force of development will weaken, and can even slowly break down, if at Marytown were found such who would have some restrictions in their dedication to the Immaculata, even though they would have the most conformable customs or prescriptions but reservations. Unreservedness of dedication in food, clothing, occupation, state and place, either in one's own native land or among enemies of the faith, where a sure death may be waiting, and so on—in brief, we are not to place *any* bounds, even if it were our lot to perish from hunger and misery in a gutter for the Immaculata.

This is the essential character of Marytown. It demands something of heroism, yet otherwise it would be difficult to attain the end of the MI.

22. Marytown is like the home of Nazareth. The father is God the Father, the mother and lady of the house is the Immaculata; the firstborn son and our brother is Jesus in the Blessed Sacrament of the Altar. All the younger brothers endeavor to imitate the older ones in love and honor towards God and the Immaculata, our common parents.

From the Immaculata they learn to love the divine big brother, our prototype, our ideal of holiness, who deigned to descend from heaven, become incarnate in her and dwell among us in the tabernacle. The whole world is a huge Marytown, where also God is the father, the Immaculata is the mother, the elder brother is Jesus in so many tabernacles over the world, and the younger brothers are the people.

Heaven is likewise a Marytown, because the same Father is there and mother and elder Brother in the flesh.

## CHAPTER 5

# The Spirit of Marytown

1. The spirit of Marytown consists in nothing else but belonging to the Immaculata. Everything in it is hers: inhabitants, machines, buildings and even the debts. Above all *every heart beating in it* belongs to her.

2. Marytown arose from offerings made to the Immaculata. It must conquer the whole world for her, or fulfill the end of the MI. To change this end would mean it had lost its reason for existence.

Marytown would lose its momentum, grow stagnant, seek its ease and corrupt.

3. It is Marytown because it belongs to the Immaculata exclusively, since it is wholly consecrated along with all the hearts beating within its confines, all the machines, motors, schools, tools, hopes, anxieties, troubles, debts. In a word, it is her property and possession.

4. Marytown would not be a real City of the Immaculata if it did not resemble the Immaculata.

5. In answer to any difficulties we can only increase our activity to win the whole world for the Immaculata.

6. As far as the general condition of the spirit at Marytown is concerned, let us on our part strive to do all we can. As for the rest let us be at ease. The Immaculata will not fail on her part to manage everything in the best way.

7. The essence of the spirit of a member of Marytown consists in the supernatural and perfect *obedience* to the Immaculata through superiors. Whoever does not desire to be perfect in this point is not suited for Marytown.

Because the self-surrender to the Immaculata at Marytown is *without restrictions*, one does not even exclude missionary work, although the Rule leaves us free on this point.

8. Among us at Marytown the deepening of the spirit of the Immaculata must be found in its fullness.

9. Let him rather leave the gates of Marytown who does not so love the Immaculata as to desire to consecrate all to her (poverty) and his entire self (obedience)—in other words, to surrender oneself unreservedly to the Immaculata to become an instrument in her hands.

## CHAPTER 6

# The Basis of Marytown

1. From the very beginning the project of the Militia depends upon and develops in obedience, and only in obedience. The very beginning of Marytown had its foundation in obedience.

The rise of the *Militia Immaculatae* and its further development depended on obedience, regardless of all plans and convictions. The transfer of the publication to Grodno, the purchase of the printing press, the transfer of the whole work of the MI to the City of the Immaculata, the foundation of a minor seminary, the beginning of the Japanese mission project—always and everywhere and in everything only obedience.

Why is it so? For, as a matter of fact, only in this way can we be sure that the Immaculata is our manager. Everything else, however prudent, wise, holy, if not in agreement with her will, does not belong to the Immaculata, but to the one who is under her feet.

2. The foundation that assures the development of Marytown is our relationship to the Immaculata. The more we are united to the Immaculata, the stronger the ties that will bind us, the more she will reign in the souls of the brothers, the stronger will be our development. And nothing else is the foundation except this interior life, this union with the Immaculata.

## CHAPTER 7

# Development of the Idea of Marytown and Its Mission

1. The essential development of Marytown is our drawing close to the Immaculata.

2. In order that Marytown develop more and more, it must belong more and more to the Immaculata in every respect.

3. The greater our inability and the stronger the obstacles, the more obvious it becomes that it is

she, the Immaculata, who alone accomplishes everything. In this admission lies the source of unusual power for developing our Militia's publication.

4. The more perfect the obedience the more will the Immaculata rule Marytown and every soul which is found within its walls. The more souls there are who give themselves perfectly to her and live this spirit of obedience, the more will the Immaculata direct her Marytown.

5. For seven centuries we have fought for the recognition of the truth of the Immaculate Conception. This struggle was crowned by the proclamation of the dogma and the apparition of the Immaculata at Lourdes.

Now is the time for the second half of the story: the dissemination of this truth in souls, care over its growth and bearing the fruit of holiness, in all souls who are and will live until the end of the world.

The first half, those seven centuries, were only a preparation, the formulation of a plan, of a motto. Only now that truth takes on flesh: the manifestation of the Immaculata to souls, her introduction into souls with all its blessed results.

6. Remember it is not sufficient that the present spirit be the same as it was at the beginning. Every

year, every day there must be progress. Marytown must belong much more to the Immaculata today than in the first days of its existence.

7. We must strive to love Jesus as Mary loved him, so that our love reach such perfection as to become the very love of the Immaculata. This is the height of love and towards this summit we must tend. We must win the whole world for that love and direct it to reach the summit.

8. Marytown arose, developed and will develop further only on the ground of religious obedience. Let all of us who live at Marytown strive to deepen this virtue of obedience more perfectly; then we will belong to the Immaculata more and more and she will rule us and the whole Marytown. Then Marytown will attain its goal. Then it will radiate and in this way will win all the more souls for her. Whoever does not wish to travel this way ought to go by an altogether different way and not to hinder us.

Only he who is an instrument of the Immaculata can cooperate. In the other case he will be an instrument of that serpent whose head she crushes under her heel. In a word, he will create confusion for us and will be an obstacle to the cause of the Immaculata.

9. The essential development of Marytown is the development of the love of God in our souls, and the continual drawing near to the Sacred Heart of Jesus through the Immaculata.

Even if the very fences of Marytown became narrower, if only our souls drew close to the Immaculata then we could say that Marytown is developing. Even if they scatter us to all parts of the world, and each one is forced to flee without the habit, but if the love of the Immaculata be developing in our souls it would even then be a real advancement for Marytown.

In this then is rooted our essential progress, that our souls become at every moment more and more the property of the Immaculata.

10. When then will the Immaculata rule over the world? When will her Marytown arise in every country and her *Knight* be translated into every language, be brought to every home, palace, hut? When will her medal be worn on every breast, and every heart on the globe of the earth beat for her?

I am aware of no better means of hastening this blessed moment than if everyone of us would strive more to deepen in himself his dedication to the Immaculata. The more perfectly we belong to her, the more freely will she herself be able to direct us. No activity is more efficacious.

59

11. What wouldn't I give if I could make sure that here at Marytown perfect obedience might flourish?

The printeries, the machines, its outward growth do not comprise the development of Marytown. These are secondary matters. The essential thing is that each soul be united with the Immaculata, our will with her will, our understanding with hers, so that she would act in us as she will.

This is the secret of the rise and whole progress of the MI, and it will be the pledge of the future progress of its activity.

## CHAPTER 8

# Director of the Central Office of the MI

The director of the Central Office of the MI ought to deepen his knowledge in matters pertaining to the Immaculata, and then he is to radiate it about.

## CHAPTER 9

# The Philosophy of Marytown

1. The most intimate drawing near to the Immaculata is the whole philosophy of Marytown. Everything else is secondary and has importance only as it leads to the goal of Marytown.

2. Our purpose is to fulfill God's will, the will of the Immaculata. Other goals are a waste of time.

61

## CHAPTER 10

# The Knight of the Immaculata

1. The Knight of the Immaculata does not confine his heart to himself, nor to his family, relatives, neighbors, friends, or countrymen, but embraces the whole world, each and every soul, because without exception they have all been redeemed by the blood of Jesus. They are all our brothers. He desires true happiness for everyone, enlightenment in faith, cleansing from sin, inflaming their heart with love of God, a love without restriction. The happiness of all mankind is in God and through the Immaculata. Behold this is the dream of the Knight of the Immaculata.

2. Therefore, my child,

(a) Love her generously as a mother. She loves you even to the sacrifice of the Son of God. At the Annunciation she accepted you willingly as her child.

(b) She will make you like herself, more and more immaculate; she will nourish you with the milk of her grace. Allow her only to lead you more freely and to mold you. Watch over the purity of your conscience, cleanse it in her love. Do not become discouraged even after a mortal sin, even committed many times. An act of perfect love will cleanse you.

(c) Property and possession: May she do with you what pleases her. Let us not bind her with any restrictive obligations of mother toward child. Be her property, her possession. Freely permit her to exhaust you in any way she please, without any restrictions.

Your owner, your lady and absolute queen: A servant sells his labor, but you should give your labor and suffering and whole self as a gift. Beg her not to respect your will, but always to act freely with you according to her will.

Be her child and servant and slave out of love in every single respect which anyone has or ever will express or be able to discover. *In a word, be hers.*

Become a Knight that others become hers more and more, as you yourself and even more than yourself. Let your goal be everyone who is and will be on the entire globe, and who will cooperate with her in the fight with the serpent.

3. Our greatest mission is to show by our practical life how a Knight of the Immaculata looks.

4. At every moment I am ready to depart anywhere for the missions if only the Immaculata should wish it through holy obedience.

5. We are not only "I" (of the Immaculata), her property, but likewise "M" (Militia-men), her Knights. Therefore to battle for souls!

6. We are Knights of the Immaculata ready for any expedition, any place, any time.

7. Suffer in knightly fashion, labor and die, but not by an ordinary death—perhaps by a bullet in the head, in order to seal your love towards the Immaculata. In such knightly fashion pour out your blood to the last drop to hasten the conquest of the whole world for her.

8. The Knights of the Immaculata are so called a knighthood because a member does not restrict himself to his own consecration to the Immaculata, but strives as much as he is able to cause other hearts to give themselves to her, as he has done. He strives to win countless hearts for her, the hearts of all those who are and ever will be until the end of the world.

9. A soul belonging to the knighthood of the Immaculata ceases to disquiet itself even over its own eternity. It acknowledges that everything that does not depend upon its own will comes from the hand of God through the Immaculata. For the soul's part it strives to do all it can to know the will of the Immaculata more perfectly, and more faithfully fulfill it, at the cost of great suffering and

even at the sacrifice of blood.

10. The Knight of the Immaculata is not indifferent to the spread of evil, but hates it with his whole heart and wars against every evil that poisons human souls on every occasion, in every place and at every time.

11. There is no kind of heroism which a soul cannot achieve with the help of the Immaculata.

12. To suffer, labor and die for God alone, through the Immaculata as an instrument in her hand, is the ideal worthy of a Knight of the Immaculata.

13. The Knight of the Immaculata knows that in the Immaculata and through her he will most rapidly and easily belong to Jesus—become God's. He knows that she loves Jesus in him and through him without comparison more perfectly than he himself would try to do with every other means.

He knows that just as every grace flows into his soul from God the Father through Jesus and the Immaculata, so every response to that grace, every repayment of love for love can and should rise in no other way than through her and Jesus to the Father.

14. He knows that it is the only way to the easiest and most sublime sanctity, to the greatest glory of God. By becoming more and more the

Immaculata's, even to the knightly conquest of an ever-growing mass of souls by belonging to Jesus through the Immaculata, and by belonging more perfectly to the Father in heaven through Jesus, the soul becomes more of a Knight of the Immaculata and penetrates more deeply into the essence of the *Militia Immaculatae*.

15. It is not enough to become the Immaculata's within some defined limit. In every respect we must desire to radiate her, so as to draw to her the souls of all others who are, will be and might be— without restriction. In a word, we are to become hers more and more ready to sacrifice self entirely for her, to the last drop of blood in the conquest of the whole world and every soul in particular—for her and as soon as possible, as soon as possible, as soon as possible.

16. He who has known the Immaculata, loved her, dedicated himself to her so completely that he left nothing for himself and did not make any reservations; he who strives to belong more and more to her under every aspect; he who in his solicitude for her kingdom in souls desires that others dedicate themselves to her and on his part does all he can towards this goal and strives not to omit any means, even if it cost him very much and even if it would come to sealing this ideal with blood—such

a person is a perfect Knight of the Immaculata. He considers it the greatest happiness, the culminating point of his dreams to make a total sacrifice of his own life for the conquest of all souls for her. This includes all men wherever they are, to whatever nations or race they belong, and whenever they live now or in the future—he is a perfect Knight of the Immaculata.

## CHAPTER 11

# The Miraculous Medal

1. Because conversion and sanctification are divine graces, the Miraculous Medal will be the best means for reaching our purpose. For that reason it constitutes a first rate weapon of the Knights; it is the bullet with which a faithful soldier cuts down the enemy, that is, evil, and thus rescues souls.

2. Let us contribute all our strength in bringing about what was already foreseen by St. Catherine Laboure, to whom the Immaculata graciously revealed the Miraculous Medal, that the Immaculata be queen of the whole world and of each soul in particular as soon as possible.

## CHAPTER 12

# The Statue of the Immaculata

1. May the statue of the Immaculata, dominating every workshop, every cell of Marytown, help us often to remind ourselves during the day about our obligation as children of turning to her before the more important actions.

2. In order to show a greater love towards the Immaculata, we can make an agreement with her whereby, for example, a glance at her statue, a difficulty, an ejaculation, some labor, will be a renewal of our dedication to her.

## CHAPTER 13

# The Apostolate

1. Love does not rest, but spreads like fire consuming everything. All of us, members of the MI, must endeavor to be penetrated with these flames of love, so that this fire inflame all souls who are and will be in the world.

2. Let us pray, bear little crosses, greatly love the souls of all our neighbors without exception,

friends or enemies. Let us have confidence in this one goal, that she become the queen of each and every soul in particular in the whole world as soon as possible.

3. Every trip outside the cloister, every trip to Warsaw or elsewhere ought to be our sermon. The more we sanctify ourselves, the more effective will be our apostolate, which is to flow out from our interior abundance.

4. The shortest way of saving a soul is to inspire it to accomplish or suffer at least something, if even the slightest, for the Immaculata, the most gracious queen of heaven and earth by the will of Almighty God.

5. The Immaculata excited in our hearts a love toward herself even to an entire dedication of ourselves to her cause, a cause to win all the more souls for her love—indeed, to help all souls to know and love her, and through her to draw near to the divine Heart of Jesus, whose love for us extended even to the cross and the tabernacle.

How then would we be able to spread our apostolate if the love in our soul, instead of being inflamed more and more, would gradually die out? Let us pray often and ardently, all for one and one for all, so that the Immaculata would protect us from that misfortune.

6. We are to lead all souls to the feet of the Immaculata. Therefore great effort and sacrifice is necessary to reach our goal as soon as possible. It is a marvelous and shining goal: *to win the whole world for the Immaculata, and through her for the most Sacred Heart of Jesus and that as soon as possible.*

To the attack, therefore. To the offensive!

7. He who spreads much honor and love towards the Immaculata, he who wins souls for her and through her for the Sacred Heart of Jesus who loved us even to the death of the cross; such a one will show the greatest love because of an active love towards the Sacred Heart of Jesus. Such a one will also be most intimately united with it.

8. Let us remember that the Immaculata repays liberally even the least showing of honor to her. Let those among whom we are spreading her kingdom at least do some little thing for her and she will never forget it.

9. Let us try not to weaken in the missionary work of gaining hearts for Mary. Let us pray that her reign in souls spread. Let us offer our afflictions and troubles for this purpose and let us try above all things to be pleasing to her. We shall reach this goal, if our conscience is always pure.

10. In laboring for souls we must give our ut-

most. The fuller the vessel of our apostolate, the more it will overflow upon other souls.

11. Inasmuch as the evil spirit does not wait, but acts quickly and according to plan, we *cannot* for whatever motives *stop in our activities* at Marytown. The question here concerns souls and the conquering of the whole world and every soul in particular for the Immaculata, for the sanctification of all souls through the Immaculata, even to the end of the world. The loss of even one soul is a misfortune.

12. Of ourselves we are capable of nothing, but with the aid of the Immaculata we will convert the whole world; we will throw the whole world at her feet! Let us only be hers in entirety and without restriction.

13. Let us live by the love of the Immaculata, let us labor for her love and so radiate love to others.

14. It is surely the will of God that the Immaculata win all souls. We can offer without restriction all our hardships, inconveniences and sufferings to the Immaculata for this intention, that she conquer the world.

15. It does not matter whether I or another person do more for the cause of the Immaculata, but that as much as possible be accomplished. May she as soon as possible and as perfectly as possible

possess every soul and live in it, act in it, and love the divine Heart of Jesus. It is a question of unreserved and more and more intensive strengthening of the love of a creature towards his Creator.

16. You of little faith, why does doubt steal into your heart?

Stir up love and confidence toward Mary Immaculate everywhere. You will soon see tears flowing from the eyes of the most hardened sinners, prisons will be emptied, the ranks of earnest workers will increase, and the family hearths will give a pleasant odor of virtue, peace and happiness will destroy discord and pain, because then it will be a *new era*.

### CHAPTER 14

# Missions and Cities of the Immaculata

1. In every country there must arise a City of the Immaculata, and we must win every soul and all organizations for the Immaculata.

2. If anyone at Marytown were to deliberate whether or not he is called to the missions, let him

recall that he who has really dedicated himself to the Immaculata wholly and without any condition cannot place any restrictions over this dedication.

So also as the missions are concerned. He ought to do whatever is necessary, as far as it depends on him, so that the Immaculata might through holy religious obedience call him at any moment, wherever it will please her, regardless of whether it be a Catholic country or a pagan one.

3. It seems to me that all the Cities of the Immaculata of each particular country will constitute one whole, intimately united, one world army, continually fighting without ceasing until the end of the world, so that even though "She shall crush thy head," nonetheless "thou shalt lie in wait for her heel." Thus to the end of the world the devil will not cease to tempt, confuse, free himself and make war. He will be only as strong as the Immaculata permits, or as much as is necessary for the gathering up of merits, with our victory always certain, if under her banner, with her and for her and in her.

4. We love our closest neighbors, but do we have a place in our hearts for the poor souls, tangled in the snares of heresy or schism? Let us open our hearts to them and let us try to introduce the Immaculata into their poor hearts, so that she bring

them true happiness, God.

5. In the missions you will encounter not only outward difficulties, but God, for his greater glory and to show the goodness and power of the Immaculata, will allow still more, that you will undergo dissatisfaction, doubt, intense longing and the like. Nevertheless do not trust in yourself at all, but place your entire confidence in the Mediatrix of All Graces, our dearest mother, the Immaculata. You will always and certainly be victorious, even if all hell, the flesh and the devil should conspire against you. Then not only you yourself will not succumb, but you will have enough strength to comfort others and refresh their spirit, reminding them to whom they are to turn for light and strength.

6. Strengthen the offensive of prayer for the cause of a third Marytown. Some say a fourth, because not without reason do they assert that a Marytown already exists in heaven, where the Immaculata is guardian, and the workers are Father Fordon, Father Venanty, Father Alphonse, Brother Albert and so on.

7. Would that the Immaculata herself rule in her own City of the Immaculata and in the Cities of the Immaculata on the whole earth.

8. It would not be right to forget that not only

Poland and Japan exist under the sun, but many more hearts beat beyond the boundaries of these countries. When will the Knights of the Immaculata come to them? When will they establish Cities of the Immaculata in their lands? When will they lead them to the Sacred Heart of Jesus upon the white ladder of the Immaculata, which our holy father Francis saw?

9. We feel very happy that our dear Immaculata bestowed on us the grace to work for her, at times even to grow fatigued by these little sacrifices and help towards the salvation of poor pagans (in Japan). There are moments when the soul longs for the Polish Marytown. But these are only passing moments, for when we consider that we will meet in heaven, a joyous zeal and desire to destroy oneself for God enters the heart.

10. When will we fix the standards of the Immaculata in her Cities of the Immaculata upon the other hemispheres: in Canada, the United States, Mexico, various republics of Central America, Brazil, Argentina, Chile, Peru, Bolivia and so on? Would that the Immaculata deign to hasten that moment.

11. The activity of the MI and the Cities of the Immaculata, both present and future over the entire earth, must be intimately united, because this

is *one* spirit and *one* body. Otherwise there will be no vigor.

12. In every City of the Immaculata, Polish or Japanese or any other, wherein great zeal will flourish, many devils will also attack it. And on the contrary, where there will be relaxing of discipline the attacks of the devils will lessen in the same degree.

13. All the Cities of the Immaculata have a common purpose.

14. How little known is the Immaculata, both theoretically and still less in practical life! How many prejudices, misunderstandings and difficulties wander about in the minds of men! Would that the Immaculata allow her Cities to brighten this darkness, to disperse this cold fog and to stir up and inflame love toward her freely and *without limitations, with complete freedom*, without those various misgivings that stiffen and cool the heart! Would that they look for the King, not beside the palace but in it, in its depths, in its inner chambers.

15. It seems to me, that in the Polish Marytown there will be little ground needed for a cemetery, because most of the bones will rest in various parts of the world. We shall embrace the whole world!

16. The Cities of the Immaculata of all countries of the world are a single project, one City of the

Immaculata, an army for conquering the whole world for the Immaculata in the spirit of the MI.

## CHAPTER 15

# The Name of Mary

1. The fondness of greeting each other with the name of Mary is a sign of life.

2. Such peace the holy name of Mary gives! Let us repeat it often in the depths of our soul. Let it become the breath of our heart.

3. Try to run to Mary as a little child to its best, beloved mother, if only *by invoking* the holy name of Mary with your lips or heart in the difficulties of life, in the darkness and weakness of soul. You will be convinced of what Mary is able to do and who her Son, Jesus Christ, is.

4. I came to you and said "Mary," and you answered me "Mary," likewise. Such is the custom at Marytown that upon meeting each other we greet one another with the name of Mary.

5. As soon as the soul notices that it has lost itself in work, it is necessary to make contact with the Immaculata anew, if only by sighing "Mary!"

6. The name of Mary must permeate everyone at Marytown.

**PART THREE**
# RELIGIOUS LIFE

# CHAPTER I

# Religious Vows

1. Remember well, dear children, that the certain and single condition for living up to all the vows is the love for the Immaculata. It is a necessary condition, because through her all graces flow upon us. Religious life will be easy for whomever goes by this way.

2. Who must keep the vows?

We ourselves. No one will substitute for us in this, not even God himself. We ourselves make our vows consciously and we ourselves are to fulfill what we vow.

3. We must all be watchful, because we are not able to keep the vows of our own strength. We need grace with which we must cooperate.

## Obedience

1. Obedience is the will of God, the will of the Immaculata.

2. For fulfilling the will of God, we can do noth-

ing more perfect, since even Jesus himself, if he were in our place, could do nothing more perfect than what we are doing according to the precepts of the Order or wishes of the superiors. It is another matter if one considers the manner of Jesus' obedience, which was infinitely more perfect.

3. Religious obedience ought to be observed only with an eye to God, since all human beings are equal and obeying someone for his own sake is degrading to a man.

4. Not in mortification, not in prayer, not in labor, not in rest, but in obedience is the essence and merit of holiness.

5. The perfection of obedience is the perfection of our love of the Immaculata.

6. In order to be sanctified in an Order, it is sufficient to fulfill exactly the will of God in everything. He fulfills the will of God who is really blindly obedient to his superiors.

7. We are not to obey the superior because he is learned, experienced, prudent, pleasant, amiable, etc., but because obedience is the will of God, the will of the Blessed Mother.

8. Through obedience we rise above our finitude and we act according to the infinite wisdom, the wisdom of God.

9. There is one indication whereby one recog-

nizes whether a soul is advancing in perfection and is drawing near to the Immaculata, and this is obedience.

10. He is not a good religious who does much or little, but one who performs as exactly as possible whatever is commanded him, in other words, when he fulfills the will of God.

11. Obedience and only obedience reveals the will of God to us.

12. Love, love without bounds toward our best Father is that love which exhibits and exercises itself through obedience, especially when it is a question of doing what does not please us.

13. Religious obedience is as it were a mystery of the Faith.

As in the Sacred Host, though I see only an ordinary wafer, still I firmly believe that the true God is under its veil, both Soul and Body. So also, in holy obedience, though I see only a human being in the superior, nevertheless I believe that Christ commands and acts in his person—he who said, "He who hears you, hears me."

14. Through obedience we become infinitely powerful. For who can resist the will of God?

15. We are instruments in the hands of the Immaculata in regard to the MI. Therefore we ought to accomplish only what she herself desires.

And this is evident through obedience.

16. Let us beware lest we do anything in the MI beyond that which obedience permits, because then we would not act as an instrument in the hands of the Immaculata.

17. Dear brethren, be blindly obedient in every instance if you wish that God's intention in your regard be fulfilled.

18. A careless religious loses the vitality of faith in the will of God, which is in religious obedience.

19. Whatever we perform by obedience is a great thing.

20. By obedience the *Knight of the Immaculata* appeared, by obedience we transferred the publication from Kracow to Grodno, by obedience Marytown arose, by obedience we set out after a time for the missions and by obedience we shall fulfill even other plans of the Immaculata.

21. One should be obedient, willingly and joyfully, proving he is truly dedicated to the Immaculata, and not such an indifferent servant who says, "where they place me, there I'll be." But one acts with energy and effort to fulfill the work entrusted to him as best as possible.

Even if the world be falling into ruins, regardless of what educated and holy people may wisely teach us, let us always do what the Immaculata desires of us. All minds are finite, no matter how great their genius; all minds will always fit into a hat. But the wisdom of the Immaculata, or the wisdom of God, is infinite.

22. We need not look for extraordinary mortifications, fasting, sleeping on boards, wearing chains, scourging oneself to blood, or spending whole days in prayer, reading pious books, but our only task is to fulfill the will of God through perfect obedience.

23. We must endeavor to exhibit obedience in practice. This includes obedience to rules, obedience to superiors, obedience to statutes of the Order.

24. Only holy obedience is able to reveal infallibly the will of God, the will of the Immaculata. The perfection of the virtue of obedience to superiors is a practical knighthood of the Immaculata, a living MI. This does not mean that one should have no initiative. On the contrary, one can and must freely tell his superiors the thoughts and desires of his heart, provided he is ready with calm resignation of will (for nature at times can be averse) to accept the decision of obedience, whether it is according to, against or beyond our desire.

25. What I would not give to make sure that

Marytown will always have that supernatural, regular obedience, without respect for the superior, whether he is old or young, experienced or not. Then I will be at peace to know that the Immaculata will rule Marytown.

26. The superiors should diligently watch that they do not give the impression of their superiority in their orders and wishes.

Absolute equality should distinguish us all, since in the eyes of the infinite God we are all equal, and only our occupations, as parts in a theatrical production, are varied.

27. Brother superiors, if it is the will of the Immaculata that you fulfill the duty of a superior in some division of the work, you should very peacefully accept it and carry its burden willingly. From the instant you place it on your back through holy obedience, God always grants the necessary graces.

28. The superior must pray quite a bit for his subjects. He must beg for grace for himself and for them. With love and goodness, determination and gentleness, let him try to gain souls and draw them close to the Immaculata.

## Poverty

*The Immaculata* is our goal and poverty is our capital: these are two things that Marytown may not desert *under any condition*. Without this goal it would cease to be Marytown, *it would become unfaithful* to its task. Without poverty and dependence upon the providence of God there is no place or talk about progress.

## Chastity

1. A powerful incentive for protecting oneself from an unchaste sin is the remembrance of death.

Dear children, endeavor to draw closer and closer to the Immaculata. With her help your souls will preserve their angelic whiteness and will rise to the heights of holiness.

2. In a cloister the loss of a religious vocation begins with sensual immodesty. If a fallen soul is found among others, he infects them, and that is why it is necessary to remove him immediately.

3. Every day let us become more ideal instruments in the hands of the Immaculata through the cleansing of the soul and through great delicacy,

especially regarding the vow of chastity. Whenever we have a little time, let us devote ourselves more to prayer, begging for the graces necessary to work on our soul—for the grace that the Immaculata change us and make us her Knights.

## CHAPTER 2

# The Grace of God and Holiness

1. Conversion and sanctification are the fruits of grace, and we must cooperate with that grace. Without the grace of God our holy father Francis did not attempt to perform works of conversion.

2. Deepening of the interior life is the essence of the religious state, and exterior things are only an indication, an effect of interior perfection.

3. For flowers of virtue to blossom in our soul, they must be heated by the warmth of the Immaculata.

Just as a child understands and instinctively feels it will be nurtured near its mother, so does the soul develop near the Mother of God. It must be nursed at her breast in order to live.

4. A certain specialization and stabilization is a good thing. But if that were dearer to someone than

the sanctification of a soul, it would be necessary to throw this whole specialization and stabilization far away.

5. Souls who know the Immaculata more intimately and love her more ardently strenuously endeavor to make their consciences more pure and delicate, in order to resemble her all the more, be pleasing to her, bring her pleasure.

6. The whole value of a religious depends on his interior, supernatural life.

7. The more one is in contact with the Immaculata, the more abundant will his interior life be.

8. Let the soul turn often to the Immaculata, and it will see how all other attachments begin to weaken.

9. Not even the wisest precepts sanctioned by the severest penalties will suffice to regenerate the Order. Supernatural grace is necessary—the sanctification of the religious.

Since the Mediatrix of All Graces is the Immaculata, the closer one draws to her, the more abundant will be his spiritual life.

10. There is no sin so horrible that would not threaten us were it not that the grace of God or the merciful hand of the Immaculata would not support us.

11. The act of fulfilling God's will is love and love is the essence of holiness.

12. You live once, not twice. Become a saint and not by halves, but wholly, for the greater glory of the Immaculata and through her for the glory of God. Our holiness will praise the Blessed Mother, and the Immaculata will praise God, just as an artist's picture praises the painter and the master who taught him.

13. Do you know that:

— the Immaculata can also perform miracles?

— that St. Therese of the Child Jesus hands a martyr's palm to a missionary for the very reason that he became a missionary?

— that in a little while we shall stand at the gates of eternity, where a generous reward awaits us for every labor, every suffering?

— that everyone can become a saint, and a great saint, with the aid of the Immaculata, if only he wills it?

14. Only the present moment is in our hands. How important then is the present moment, how important is the reminder that we are to sanctify ourselves now, not at any other time. We should sanctify ourselves at every moment, because we do not know whether the next will be ours.

15. Let us diligently guard our stainless purity

of conscience, and should it be stained, let us try to cleanse it as soon as possible.

16. Only he enjoys happiness in the cloister who has a single purpose before his eyes: the sanctification of his soul through the fulfillment of the will of God more and more perfectly with the help of the Immaculata.

17. We came to the Order only to sanctify ourselves. Everything else is a means, good insofar as it leads to the end.

18. I can really be a saint, if only I will it.

19. The longer we are in the Order, the more perfect we are to become. We must deepen religious perfection, deepen it more considerably from day to day, deepen it and deepen it still more!

20. It is necessary to sanctify oneself unconditionally, because we live only once.

21. From each individual brother I will demand that he strive to be the greatest saint possible, because he came to the cloister only for the purpose of being a saint.

22. Let us continually regenerate ourselves. When we are dying, we will still be regenerating ourselves, just as our holy father Francis. Upon this constant self-regeneration depends the progress of the soul.

## CHAPTER 3

# Holy Communion and Prayer

1. There is no better preparation for Holy Communion than to entrust it all to the Immaculata. She knows best how to prepare our hearts, and thus we may be certain that we afford Jesus the greatest pleasure, that we show him the greatest love.

Even without this actual oblation we are hers, because we have dedicated ourselves to her and never revoked our dedication.

2. The Immaculata suggests a thousand ways to her children. For example, someone may desire to give her the greatest joy of which he is capable. What does he do? He borrows the most Sacred Heart of Jesus, and then he is sure that he has infinitely outrun all men and angels taken together in his love of the Immaculata. In turn, he loves Jesus with her heart, or rather she in him and through him loves Jesus, for example, in Holy Communion.

3. Prayer, prayer above all, is an effective weapon in the fight for freedom and happiness of souls.

Only supernatural means lead to a supernatural end. Heaven, or, if I may say so, the divinization of the soul, is something supernatural in the full sense of the word. With natural powers one is incapable of reaching it. One needs a supernatural means, the grace of God. One gains this grace by humble and confident prayer. Grace, and only grace, illuminating the intellect and strengthening the will, is the reason for conversion, or freeing the soul from the fetters of evil.

4. The saints claim that whoever prays to the Mother of God during a temptation will surely *not sin*. Whoever turns to her throughout life with confidence will surely be saved.

5. Much patience and confidence in the Immaculata is necessary, and much prayer in difficulties, or the invocation of the sweetest name of Mary, or "Hail Mary." In more difficult and more important situations, five decades of the Rosary will not be out of the way. Yes, every difficulty or suffering will change itself into a source of merit.

6. My dear brothers, let us remember and often recall that a single turning to the Immaculata will suffice, either by word or glance or only a thought, so that she would repair all that we have ruined both in ourselves and those around us. She will guide us at the present moment and take our future and the results of our future work under her

care. For that reason let us often have recourse to her.

7. The entire fruit of our activity in the direction of converting and sanctifying souls depends upon prayer.

8. Without regard for what kind of sins we have on our conscience, we can rise from them if only we turn with all confidence to the Immaculata.

9. The cause of the Immaculata is to be our activity. We *cannot permit* that other purposes displace our main purpose: *to win the whole world for the most Sacred Heart of Jesus through the Immaculata.* Everything must measure up to that purpose, because these are *divine* affairs. Here we need to get on our knees, with the attitude that all prayer, ejaculations, all our imperfections are to be burned for her, so that we love her, draw near to her, throw out from ourselves what is not hers.

10. One who cannot bend his knees and beg her in humble prayer to know who she is, let him not expect to learn anything more intimate about her.

11. You know the story of the prayer of Duns Scotus: "Permit me to praise you, O Most Holy Virgin; give me strength against your enemies."

We see how the first part of this prayer is humble: "Permit me to praise you." But in the second part we see how strong and resolute it is: "give me strength against your enemies." Hence the second part of the prayer is strength and manliness, strength against one's enemies.

12. Prayer is not for prayer's own sake, but to help us unite our will with the will of God. Always and everywhere prayer is necessary, but as a means, not an end.

13. We are to win the whole world for the Immaculata; therefore we must strongly support ourselves by prayer.

14. If anyone is physically weak, he must nourish himself better and more often. In the same way those spiritually sick need more of the nourishment of grace, which can be obtained through prayer.

15. Let us always remember that we will know the Immaculata more in humble prayer and in the loving experiences of daily life, than from learned definitions, distinctions and arguments, even though we are not allowed to ignore these.

16. A soul without the spirit of prayer may be convinced that it does much, but it is like a ship that sails very rapidly in order to break itself on a rock.

17. I have experienced that prayer only obtains the grace of conversion.

18. Pray with short ejaculations, if only by the name of Mary. Suffer, especially by bearing what

she deigns to send whether inwardly or outwardly. Be glad, yet be glad and work and take your rest. Offer everything, everything that falls to your lot in any way, according to those intentions that especially please the Immaculata.

19. In order to subjugate nature and subdue it to the rule of the spirit, grace is necessary. That is why we must often return to prayer.

20. Let us often make ejaculations, if only by a single word, "Mary." Therefore it is a question of looking up to the Immaculata. When we take advantage of this support we will feel so powerful that no opposition will conquer us, nor drive us away from our goal.

21. Ejaculations support and cleanse the soul, as well as increase grace. Many are the ejaculations that one can make during the day and upon awakening at night. Ejaculations are very important in the spiritual life; they affect the soul, just as pieces of wood thrown into a stove affect the fire.

22. In the 'Angelic Salutation' we say, "blessed are thou among women and blessed is the fruit of thy womb, Jesus." We first say "blessed art thou," and then "the fruit of thy womb." First the rung, afterwards the ladder, the summit.

23. At Lourdes the Immaculata fingered the beads of the Rosary and thereby encouraged

Bernadette to recite it. This is a profound lesson how we are to sound the mysteries of Jesus from his coming to earth until he crowned her as Queen of Heaven, she who was his mother. Behold, if we desire to rise even to her knowledge and loving of Jesus, we must whisper "Hail Mary," and repeating it, meditate upon these mysteries in union with her.

24. With prayer to the Immaculata upon his lips or in the depths of a heart cleansed by suffering and inflamed with the fire of love for God, whoever does what lies in his power to win as many souls as possible for Jesus through the Immaculata, to free them from the fetters of evil, to make them happy; such a one and only he will be triumphant.

## CHAPTER 4

# Humility

1. Humility is the foundation of all virtue. When it is lacking, the other virtues will also disappear.

2. The first and principle thing in pursuing the cause of the Immaculata is deep humility. We must put clearly before our eyes who we are, and who she is.

3. The more humility, the greater the certainty of persevering in the Order.

4. The more humble one is, the greater holiness will he reach.

5. The very act by which the soul turns to the Immaculata is humility.

6. When someone needs humility, let him complain to the Mother of God, just as a child complains to his mother, and the Blessed Mother will surely hear that complaint.

7. There is no pride so deep-seated that the help of the Immaculata will not root it out.

## CHAPTER 5

# The Will

1. If a soul becomes stubborn and will not be tamed, then even prayer and grace will not help and the soul will be damned. This is a mystery of free will.

2. He who persists in evil and does not want to amend himself has a bad will.

3. As many times as the soul grows careless in prayer, the will at once begins to weaken.

4. We can arrive at a high degree of holiness in the Order and aid others to sanctify themselves, if only there is good will.

## CHAPTER 6

# Brotherly Love

1. True brotherly love does not seek its own pleasure, but only the love of our neighbor.

2. The more each of us draws near to the Immaculata, the more will we draw near to one another through her. In this love there is strength.

3. Mutual love underlies the love of God.

4. Immediate mutual forgiveness of injuries is a priceless source of grace and constitutes the law of love.

5. For the love of the Immaculata I am capable of forgiving always and entirely.

6. When we draw close to the Immaculata, we draw close to one another. When a soul begins to draw away from the Immaculata, it is reflected in his lack of love for others.

7. The ability to bear with one another—behold, the law of love.

8. Preserve harmony and love among yourselves.

9. Dear children, if love be your companion through life, and you live in mutual love, you will have a foretaste of heaven already here on earth.

Everything will pass away, faith and hope will pass away, but charity will remain. With charity we shall enter into eternal life and we shall delight in heaven with the Immaculata in love.

## CHAPTER 7

# Good Example

1. Even if we should labor very much and wear ourselves out, we do little unless we give a good example.

2. Is giving a good example an obligation? Yes! Everyone around us has the right to demand and to desire good example from us. He who acts otherwise sins not only against God, but in the presence of all his neighbors. Therefore he is the occasion of another's sin.

3. Let those who are older in vocation try to form the younger by example, prayer and word.

4. In the cloister one influences another very strongly, either in a good direction or in an evil, injurious way. At times, one occurrence, one good example rouses another soul and awakens it to a new life or strengthens that life still more.

## CHAPTER 8

# Silence

1. According to the judgment of the holy fathers and masters of spiritual life, silence is the mainstay and foundation of a deep interior life.

2. How does one practice silence intelligently? Above all, pray, because only the Immaculata herself can effect all this in us.

3. Silence is necessary, and even absolutely necessary. If silence is lacking, then grace is lacking. Then we shall cease to be instruments in the hands of the Immaculata, and we shall only spoil things, even if we should be doing the most sublime work.

4. To keep silence does not mean to say nothing, but to say only as much as the Immaculata wishes, no more, no less. To say less than is necessary is evil, and to say more than necessary is also evil.

5. It is proper continually to keep watch over oneself, so that we say only what is essential and necessary for settling our business.

6. If we do not observe the prescribed silence, then we will not be able to correspond with grace. If we do not correspond to one grace, a whole series of graces will be lost to us, which we might have received if we had kept our recollection.

7. A recollected soul, faithfully observing silence, listens to the inspirations and holy direction from the Holy Spirit, who speaks only in the quiet heart and draws it to himself.

8. If we observe silence well, we shall be regenerated inwardly.

# CHAPTER 9

# Peace

1. To fulfill the will of the Immaculata means to feel a great interior peace and untroubled happiness already here on earth.

2. The source of peace is resignation to the will of God: to do what is in our power and leave the rest to the care of divine providence and have the confidence of a child toward its best Mother.

3. Let us not lose peace when our sensible affection grows cold. It is a question of the will and only of the will.

## CHAPTER 10

# Fidelity

1. A real and complete satisfaction of the spirit can be had by one whose conscience bears witness to the fact that he is faithfully fulfilling the will of God and never bends away from it.

2. We should always strive for peace and for fidelity, in the least fulfillment of God's will. Jesus said, "My peace I give you, my peace I leave unto you."

3. All our actions must be such that the Immaculata does not have to be ashamed of them.

4. Let us love the Immaculata in a practical way through fulfilling all our duties well, from morning till night, because this is her will, the will of Jesus.

## CHAPTER 11

# Punctuality

The first occasion for punctuality during the course of the day is in the morning, when the rising bell sounds. Whoever is punctual at the first instant will be punctual the whole day. Whoever lingers for even a few seconds in rising does not receive from God those graces that he would have received, were he faithful to the first punctuality of the day.

## CHAPTER 12

# Intention

1. The perfection of every action depends on the perfection of our intention.

2. One acts and suffers everything joyfully for the Immaculata. Regardless of the unpleasantness we meet in life, let us accept all with the intention of strengthening our love toward the Immaculata.

## CHAPTER 13

# Suffering

1. Notwithstanding its being paved at times with crosses and sufferings, the way of the Immaculata is not so difficult, so dark, so unclear that we can always feel her motherly warmth.

2. A cross consists of two pieces of wood, crossed at one point. In every day life our cross consists in our will crossing the will of God. In order to remove it, it is necessary to conform ourselves to the will of God. In practice it is necessary that we put off our own will.

3. The saints did not understand life without suffering.

4. Suffering for love nourishes love.

5. Let us not always wish to feel the sweetness of devotion to the Immaculata, for this would be spiritual greed. Let us permit her to direct us as it pleases her. It is not always time for sweet caresses, be they ever so holy. We also need the *trials of dryness, abandonment* and the like. Let her fit the means to our sanctification according to her will. We must have one quality, continually deepening it: allowing ourselves to be led by her, reconciling ourselves to her will ever more perfectly, giving obedience to her will by religious obedience.

6. Whoever in life strives to avoid crosses as much as possible and does not mortify himself in anything does not know what happiness is.

7. Whoever is capable of suffering much for love can be happy that his love is deep.

8. As the harvest is a period of the farmer's greatest efforts in gathering the crops into barns and

storerooms, so also the soul's harvest is the time in which it can gather for itself as many priceless merits as possible; these are the moments pregnant with suffering and the cross.

9. If God visits us with a painful suffering and our soul walks the thorny path, it behooves us to rejoice that God destines us for high perfection.

10. God exhibits a special love for those whom he chastises in this life, because the punishment of purgatory is both long and severe. In this life the voluntary acceptance of crosses merits us an even greater glory in heaven. Hence the saying, "Whom God loves he chastises."

11. The more powerful and courageous a soul becomes with the help of God's grace, the greater the cross God places on its shoulders, so that it might mirror as closely as possible the image of the crucified in its own life.

12. We will lay up so many more graces if, while in external and internal darkness, full of sadness, overworked, suffering, without consolation, persecuted at every step, amidst continual failures, abandoned by everyone, ridiculed, alone—just as Jesus on the cross—we shall pray for everyone and strive in all ways to draw everyone to God through the Immaculata and unite them to him as intimately as possible.

13. If a sailor wants to sail against the current, he must continually row, otherwise the current will push him back. When we become tired, when it is hard for us, let us go to the Mother of God with greater confidence so that she will help us. And always, always forward, so as to fulfill the will of the Immaculata better and better.

14. Suffering and sacrifice are the proofs of love, although suffering itself is not the essence of love.

15. Without sacrifice there is no love. Sacrifice the senses, especially the eyes, particularly when one goes out of the cloister among lay people. The same can be said of taste, of hearing and so on.

16. In case of difficulties, confide them to the Immaculata, that she do with them what she pleases: remove them, lessen them, increase them or leave them without change.

17. Difficulties, no matter how great, ought never disturb us, but they should on the contrary strengthen and steel our will in the direction to overcome these same difficulties.

18. When the most varied temptations, trials befall the soul; when it is abandoned and plunged into spiritual darkness; when it as it were hangs upon the cross without respite and consolation, after the pattern of Jesus crucified, and in spite of this, with the help of God's grace peacefully and

joyously received and bears this cross even for a long time: this is *true perfection*. A soul cannot imagine to what great heights it rises and what a great glory God is preparing for it in heaven.

19. When love encompasses and penetrates us, sacrifices become necessary for the soul.

20. Spiritual joy is born of sacrifice.

21. Let us remember that love lives and nourishes itself on sacrifices. Let us thank the Immaculata for interior peace and for the exaltation of love, but let us not forget that all this, however good and beautiful, is not as it were the essence of love. Without all of this love can exist, and even a perfect love. Love's summit is the state in which Jesus on the cross said, "My God, my God, why hast thou forsaken me?"

22. Although storms rage around us often and thunder resounds, if we are unreservedly dedicated to the Immaculata we can be sure that nothing will happen to us as long as our best and dearest mother will not allow it. We shall rest sweetly as we labor and suffer for the salvation of souls.

Crosses may overwhelm us, but the grace of God, having warmed our hearts, will inflame them with such love that we will burn with the desire of suffering, of suffering without bounds, of humiliations, mockery, abandonment. Thus we will show

how we love the Father and our best friend Jesus and his dearest Immaculate Mother. For suffering is the school of love.

23. What peace and happiness will penetrate us on our deathbed to know that we have much, very much toiled and suffered for the Immaculata.

## CHAPTER 14

# Penance

1. Penance and prayer are the ordinary ways of obtaining graces.

2. Everyone who wants to be saved must do penance.

3. The most important penance is the good and faithful fulfillment of one's daily occupations.

4. The Immaculata purifies us through penance. Let us strive to deepen the spirit of penance.

5. "Penance, penance, penance," the Immaculata repeated to Bernadette. Is not this the purpose of our Order—the Order of penitents? Is it not therefore proper for us above all to take up this calling of the Immaculata and to disseminate it over the whole earth, and for all times? Let us not forget that such is her calling.

But how shall we do penance? Health and obligations do not permit the austerities of penance to all. Nevertheless all admit that their road of life is covered with crosses and the acceptance of these crosses in the spirit of penance is a wide field for the practice of penance.

Beyond the fulfillment of obligations, fulfillment of God's will in every moment of life, and fulfilling it perfectly in deed and word and thought, demands much denial of what appears more pleasant at the given moment.

Behold the most bountiful source of penance.

## CHAPTER 15

# Temptations

1. Every temptation conquered is reason for a new crown.

2. It is necessary that there be temptations. Without an enemy there will be no fight, without a fight there will be no victory, and without victory there will be no reward. We need only never acquiesce, knowingly and willingly, to the least evil.

3. Satan tempts in the cloister oftener and more

intensively than elsewhere because he knows a soul in religion will do much good not only for itself, but also for others, whom it helps with its prayers.

4. It is a common tactic of Satan to represent sin as a small evil before its commission, and afterwards to push us into despair.

5. In temptations it is necessary to beware of sin as the greatest evil. After a fall we must not forget that the Immaculata will never abandon us, for she is the Refuge of Sinners.

6. The saints say that if anyone doubts whether he consented to a temptation, he can be sure that there was no consent if he was calling on the name of the Blessed Mother. It was a victory and it will have its reward.

7. Do you know why the devil strikes at the honor of the Blessed Mother? Because he wants to snap the bond between God and us. If the devil slipped up in paradise, maybe it was a question more of the Mother of God than of Jesus.

Not to wish to acknowledge the Mother of God is human pride, dictated by the devil.

8. There must be temptations and opposition on earth; there must be labor to gain heaven.

## CHAPTER 16

# Falls

1. If a soul dedicates itself to the Immaculata, the devil will not be able to harm it in any way. And if it happens to fall, it will easily rise and the fall will become for it a stepping-stone to a still higher perfection.

2. The Immaculata can turn even our weaknesses to greater good. This is my only consolation.

3. In case of a fall never be sad, because this is stinking pride. Rise immediately and go forward with great love and joy of spirit! Repair the fall with a perfect act of love.

4. Even if someone is convinced that he is strong, let him take heed not to fall, as St. Peter fell.

5. My dearest ones, let every fall, even the worst and most habitual, serve as a rung always toward higher perfection. The Immaculata permits the fall only to cure us of our self-love, our pride, to bring us to humility and so make us more receptive to God's graces.

## CHAPTER 17

# Admonitions and Councils

1. We must be on guard against one thing most in life, namely, not to draw away from the Mother of God.

2. He who fails to have recourse to the Immaculata falls lower and lower.

3. Even if Satan leads a soul to fall very low but fails to uproot its desire to honor the Immaculata, his spoils will always be uncertain. Should some soul forget its heavenly mother and cease to give her honor, even if it employed innumerable devotions, even if it would practice all virtues possible, it will tumble inevitably into the abyss after stopping up this channel of grace.

4. My dear children, if you desire to live and die happily, strive to deepen that childlike love toward our best heavenly mother.

5. The longer a religious remains outside his cloister without necessity, the more he becomes like his surroundings, according to the saying, "Tell me who your friends are, and I will tell you what you are." Satan spares no effort to find a thousand reasons to delay the return of a soul to surroundings favorable to fidelity in keeping its vows.

6. If under any pretext, of even the greatest devotion, something would be drawing you away from the Mother of God, suspect it as a trick, even if it seems more holy. In her and through her we most surely get to the heart of Jesus. A beautiful illustration of this is our holy father Francis' vision of two ladders, red and white, upon which the brothers were climbing to heaven.

7. I am apprehensive lest the enemy inspire the brothers at some time to desert the white ladder our holy father Francis saw, and try to climb to heaven upon the red one. Satan knows what the result will be ahead of time.

8. The Immaculata will lead us to a high perfection if we cooperate with her grace.

9. Just as an iron cools when it is taken from the fire, so also souls of religious cool when among the people of the world.

10. If you hold together strongly *beside the Immaculata, you will resist* every influence foreign to the idea of Marytown.

11. Dear children, do me this favor that even after my death you do not smoke or drink liquor. Refuse, when anyone treats you. Do not wear your hair long or address each other in an inferior manner.

I entreat you that in none of the Cities of the

Immaculata tobacco be used because this would be a beginning of tepidity and weakening of the foundation, which is holy poverty.

12. If we ourselves will not be perfect instruments in the hands of the Immaculata, then how will we teach others?

Let us permit ourselves to be led by her, so that when others look at us they can learn how a Knight of the Immaculata, a citizen of her City, appears in the concrete. To reach that goal we are to dwell in her, think with her thoughts, so that there be no difference between her point of view and ours, just as there is no difference between her desires and the will of God.

This practical teaching to others is our fundamental task at Marytown. Radiate the Immaculata to such a degree that our presence drives others to her. In a word, a citizen of Marytown ought to belong to the Immaculata in the highest degree, and this is his special characteristic. He is to belong to the Immaculata more than anyone else.

13. As soon as the bell rings immediately follow its bidding. When foreign thoughts assert themselves push them aside calmly, but at once. Such a struggle day after day is a source of blessing for each of us, for Marytown as a whole, for Poland and for the world.

14. The greatest saints come from cloisters, but from these same cloisters come the worst damned souls, the greatest love or the greatest damnation. It cannot be otherwise.

15. Whoever does not earnestly work on himself will wander from the road to perfection. The religious life is a continual warfare. Even if we should have spent long years in the religious life, we still have to struggle.

16. In this life we must give a first-class example of how to love the Immaculata, how to sacrifice oneself unreservedly for her.

17. In time of success let us not be puffed up, but let us prepare for sudden change, for a persecution from those around us. Let us thank God for any success.

18. Dear children, do not become overly sad. The Immaculata turns everything to a greater good. Comfort one another. Strive to bear one another's faults, for this is the best love.

19. A scatterbrain always walks on a downward path of life, since it never has time to enter deeper into itself.

20. For us at Marytown it must be either high sanctity, or God forbid. It therefore behooves us to watch—to watch and pray!

21. Our greatest mission is to show how a Knight of the Immaculata appears in practical life.

22. You who are solemnly professed members are the foundation of Marytown, spiritual fathers, hence be about the business of the Immaculata *and do not leave off.*

23. The struggle with one's faults, self-sanctification—this is the "MI" of which the "I" is the most important work.

Interior life must be placed far above exterior life.

24. The laughter of religious ought to be very restrained. Excessive joviality or a hollow laugh, as they say, is the sign of great spiritual emptiness. It leads the soul to dissipation, making it difficult for it to be recollected at prayer and meditation. Hence it is also a great obstacle to an intimate union with God.

25. Storms will come in the course of a religious life, and thunder, discouragement, disgust. Let all this come, for come it must so that we would be able to gather merits for heaven. In every circumstance always draw near to the Mother of God. You may not feel this closeness, but if your will adheres to her it is enough. Pure, disinterested love shows itself in the face of contradiction.

26. Let us place our whole life with all its joys

and cares in the balance to win all souls for the Immaculata.

27. I would like to leave this one request. If you really desire sanctification, then remember that sanctification and perseverance depend on devotion to the Blessed Mother.

28. No one resembles Jesus who will not honor the Immaculata according to his example.

29. Let us love the Immaculata more every day, every moment. Let us give encouragement to others to love her as we do, and even more.

# PART FOUR
# THOUGHTS

1. God exists from all ages, without beginning, forever, without end.

2. The heart of man is too big to be filled with money, sensuality or the deceptive but intoxicating smoke of fame. It desires a higher good, without bounds and lasting eternally. Only God is such a good.

3. Man desires to be great, wise, rich, famous, happy, loving and beloved. But no happiness on this earth satisfies him. He desires more, always more. When will he finally be satisfied?

Even if the greatest good fortune meet him, as long as he recognizes its limitations, he reaches with desire beyond it and says, "If only this finitude would lose itself in infinity."

What *kind* of happiness does he desire? A happiness without limitation, without any limitation in intensity, expanse, duration and whatever else. Only God is such happiness, the infinite source of all happiness reflected in various degrees in creatures. Therefore man desires to possess God himself.

But how can one possess him? How can one unite himself with that happiness? As perfectly as possible, without limit, we have to become one with him, even him, God.

The very beautiful law of action and reaction, equal and opposite, written by the Creator on every action of the creature as a seal of the life of the Holy Trinity, also has its application here. The creature proceeding from the hand of the Omnipotent returns to him and will not rest except in him, until it becomes him. Because man's self-perfection, assimilation to God in a finite creature takes place by degrees, varied but nevertheless always finite, an unlimited time, eternity, is therefore necessary to reach the good. The creature will always be *finite*, but the space to cross *infinite*. This is the eternity of heaven.

4. With God everything, without God nothing!

5. Grace is far beyond the frailties and miseries of man.

6. God wants to draw the soul to himself through love.

7. Every man, whatever he is, whatever he possesses and can do, has received all from the Creator of the universe, that is, from God. Of himself man is nothing. In this respect precisely, each one of us is absolutely equal to each other.

8. Exactly how it will be in heaven, we will soon find out. After a hundred years surely none of us

will be walking upon this earth. Therefore it will not be long, so let us prepare ourselves well under the protection of the Immaculata.

9. A plant develops and blossoms under the influence of dew and sun. Yet there are arid trees that rot and perish more quickly under the influence of sun and moisture. So also among men. What is a source of life for one, may be a source of decay for those who do not want to live. Nature has no free will, but men have.

10. When we look at the atmosphere, it appears clean. Nevertheless how many tiny dust particles we see when a ray of the sun falls through a crack!

The more our soul is enlightened by the grace of God, the more it sees its imperfections and perceives the number of them.

11. For a conquered people, peace is a sign of complete subjection.

12. At the moment of death each one knows what is authoritative for him. Unfortunately we forget this when alive.

13. Life is motion, a tending toward a purpose.

14. The fundamental motive of every operation must be its end.

15. One does not live twice, but only once.

16. All that we are and whatever we have and are able to do we have from God, and we are at

every moment of our life at the receiving end. Continuance in existence is nothing but a continual receiving of existence.

Of ourselves we can do nothing, except only evil, which is precisely a negation of good.

17. Truth alone can be and is the solid foundation of happiness for individual beings, as well as all mankind.

18. Even if there were but two people in the world, still in no way would they be able to observe absolute equality. There are in all the world no two things entirely equal.

19. Even a minute, once it has passed, will never return. A miracle will not bring it back. As we have used it up, so will it remain for eternity. If it was badly used, a miracle will not erase it. This truth helps us to take advantage of time, of every little moment.

20. As soon as we lean upon God, we are giants.

21. How sweet will it be for us in the last hour when we will remember the labor, sufferings, humiliations borne for the Immaculata, and that these were numerous, very numerous—as many as possible.

22. Humanity will be happy only when the Immaculata will reign over the whole earth.

23. Even though one were on the brink of hell there is never a moment when he can say that everything is over with him.

24. He who advances according to the will of God is really a superman, a supernatural being who rises infinitely higher than all geniuses. Such a soul acts according to infinite goodness and power.

\* \* \*

Who would ever dare suppose that you, O Infinite Eternal God, have loved me from the ages of time and longer, that for as long as you are God you have loved me and always loved me! When I was nothingness, you already loved me. And just precisely because you loved me, O dear God, you led me out of nothingness into being!

For me you have created the star-sown heavens, the earth, the sea, the mountains, the rivers and so many beautiful things of earth.

\* \* \*

O Immaculate Virgin and Mother, with my confrere, Duns Scotus, I turn to you in humble petition: "Permit me to praise you, O Most Holy Virgin, and give me strength against your enemies."

Indeed, the human tongue is not capable of speaking of heavenly things. St. Paul rightly says,

125

"or has it entered the heart of man what God has prepared. . . ." How then can one grasp and express what God has prepared in you and through you?

*     *     *

When, O Mother Immaculate, will you become queen of all and each soul in particular?

When will all the souls in the entire world know the goodness and love of your heart toward them?

When will every soul show you its gratitude with ardent love and not by passing affection, but by total dedication of the will to you, so that you reign in each and every heart and be able to form them according to the pattern of the Sacred Heart of your Son, to make them happy, to divinize them? When will this come about?

*     *     *

With your help, as long as there is strength in us, we will fight till the last breath.

So help us, O Queen, O Lady, O best and dearest Mother!

# PART FIVE

# ACT OF CONSECRATION
### and
## EXPLANATION

We can dedicate ourselves to the Immaculata in various ways, and we can express this dedication in various words. Even an interior act of the will alone suffices, because this is the essence of the dedication of ourselves to the Immaculata.

For the sake of simplification, however, there is a short formula which embodies the spirit of the *Militia Immaculatae*.

## ACT OF TOTAL CONSECRATION TO THE IMMACULATA

O Immaculata, Queen of heaven and earth, refuge of sinners and our most loving Mother, God has willed to entrust the entire order of mercy to you. I, N . . ., a repentant sinner, cast myself at your feet humbly imploring you to take me with all that I am and have, wholly to yourself as your possession and property. Please make of me, of all my powers of soul and body, of my whole life, death and eternity, whatever most pleases you.

If it pleases you, use all that I am and have without reserve, wholly to accomplish what was said of you: "She will crush your head," and, "You alone

have destroyed all heresies in the whole world."
Let me be a fit instrument in your immaculate and
merciful hands for introducing and increasing your
glory to the maximum in all the many strayed and
indifferent souls, and thus help extend as far as
possible the blessed kingdom of the most Sacred
Heart of Jesus. For wherever you enter you obtain
the grace of conversion and growth in holiness,
since it is through your hands that all graces come
to us from the most Sacred Heart of Jesus.

V. Allow me to praise you, O sacred Virgin.
R. Give me strength against your enemies.

This act is divided into three parts: (1) an invocation; (2) a plea that she receive us as her property; (3) a plea that she deign to use us to gain other
souls for her.

# Explanation of the
# ACT OF CONSECRATION

In the invocation we first say,

### *O Immaculata*

We turn to her under this name, because she herself deigned to give us this name at Lourdes: the Immaculate Conception. God is immaculate, but God is not conceived. Angels are immaculate, but there is no conception with them. The first parents were immaculate before sinning, but neither were they conceived. Jesus was immaculate and conceived, but he was not a conception, for as God he already existed before and to him also applied the words of the name of God as revealed to Moses: "I am who am, who always is and does not begin to be." Other people are conceptions, but stained. She alone is not only conceived, but also a conception and immaculate. This name conceals many more mysteries, which will be discovered in time. Thus she indicates that the *Immaculate Conception* belongs to her in essence.

This name must be dear to her, because it signifies the first grace she received in the first moment of her existence. The first gift is the dearest one. This name is ratified by her life, because she was always unspotted. Hence she was also full of grace and God was always with her, even to the degree that she became the Mother of the Son of God.

## Queen of heaven and earth

In a family, the loving parents fulfill the will of the children as much as they are able, insofar as it is not harmful for them. So much more does God, the Creator and prototype of earthly parents, desire to fulfill the will of his creatures, insofar as it is not harmful for them, that is, insofar as it is conformable with his will. The Immaculata did not bend away from the will of God in anything. In all things she loved the will of God, loved God. Hence she is justly called the Omnipotent Beggar. She has influence upon God himself, on the entire world; she is the Queen of heaven and earth. In heaven everyone acknowledges the rule of her love. That group of the first angels that did not want to acknowledge her reign lost its place in heaven.

She is queen also of earth because she is the Mother of God himself, but she both desires and has a right to be freely acknowledged by every heart, be loved as the Queen of every heart, so that through her that heart might purify itself more, might become immaculate, similar to her heart and more worthy of union with God, with the love of God, with the Sacred Heart of Jesus.

### Refuge of sinners

God is merciful, infinitely merciful, nevertheless just and infinitely just. He cannot bear the least sin and must demand full satisfaction for it. The stewardess of the infinite value of the Precious Blood of Jesus that washes away sin. The Immaculata is the personification of God's mercy. Therefore she is rightly called the refuge of sinners, of all sinners regardless of the number and greatness of their sins—even though the sinner would think there is no more mercy left for him. Indeed, every cleansing of the soul is for her a new confirmation of her title of Immaculate Conception. The more deeply the soul is plunged into sin, the more does the power of her immaculateness show itself, by the fact that she gives snowy whiteness to such a soul.

### Our most loving Mother

The Immaculata is the mother of our entire supernatural life because she is the Mediatrix of the grace of God, hence our mother in the sphere of grace, in the supernatural sphere. She is a most loving mother, because you do not have any mother so affectionate, so loving, so godlike, so Immaculate, so wholly divine.

### God has willed to entrust the entire order of mercy to you

In a family, the father is glad at times that the mother stays his punishing hand over the child by her intercession, because justice is satisfied and mercy is shown. Not without cause is justice suspended. Similarly God, in order not to punish us, gives us a spiritual mother, whose intercession he never opposes. Hence the saints claim that Jesus reserved for himself the order of justice, giving to the Immaculata the whole order of his mercy.

In the second part of the act we say,

### I, a repentant sinner

We here admit that we are not as she, immaculate, but sinful. What is more, none of us can say that he has reached this day without sin, but feels himself guilty of much infidelity. We also say *unworthy*, because truly between an immaculate being and one soiled by sin there is in some sense an infinite difference. In all truth we acknowledge ourselves unworthy to turn to her, to pray to her, to fall at her feet, in order not to become similar to the proud Lucifer. Hence we also say,

### Cast myself at your feet, humbly imploring you to take me with all that I am and have, wholly to yourself as your possession and property

By these words we beg, we beseech the Immaculata to accept us. We offer ourselves to her entirely, in every respect, as her children, and as slaves of love, as servants, as instruments, and under every single aspect, under every title that anyone at any time might be able to express. We become hers as her *possession and property*, to use us and use us up even to complete destruction, according to her free disposition.

*Make of me, of all my powers of soul and body, of my whole life, death and eternity, whatever most pleases you*

To her we give our whole being, all the faculties of our soul, and therefore, intellect, memory and will, and all the faculties of the body— therefore, all the senses and each in particular, our strength, health or sickness. We offer her our entire life with all its experiences, pleasant, unpleasant or indifferent. We give her our death, whenever and wherever and in whatever way it befalls us. We give her our whole eternity. We expect that we will be able to belong perfectly to her, only then beyond comparison. In this way we express a desire and entreaty, so that she allows us to become hers under every aspect more and more perfectly.

In the third part of the act, we pray,

*Use all that I am and have without reserve wholly to accomplish what was said of you: "She will crush your head," and, "You alone have destroyed all heresies in the whole world"*

On the statues and pictures of the Immaculata we always see the serpent at her feet, surrounding the globe of the earth, as she crushes the head of the serpent.

Satan, soiled by sin, endeavors to soil all souls on earth. He hates her who was always unspotted. He waits for her heel in the persons of her children; she crushes his head in the fight in the person of everyone who has recourse to her. We ask her to use us if she wishes, as an instrument to crush the proud head of the serpent in unfortunate souls. Holy Scripture adds, quoting the verse mentioned above, *And you shall lie in wait for her heel.* The evil spirit really lies in wait in a special way for those who dedicate themselves to the Immaculata; he desires to insult her at least in them. His endeavor against sincerely dedicated souls always ends with his more shameful defeat, hence his fury is more violent, impotently furious.

The words, *You alone have destroyed all heresies in the whole world,* are taken from the prayers which the Church orders her priests to say about her. The Church says "heresies" and not the heretics, whom she loves, and because of this love desires to free them from the error of heresy. The Church says "all," without any exception; "alone," since "she" alone suffices. God is hers with all the treasures of grace for the conversion and sanctification of souls. No corner of the earth is excluded in the whole world. In this act of consecration we beg her to use us to destroy the whole serpent coiled about the earth, the serpent representing the various heresies.

*Let me be a fit instrument in your immaculate and merciful hands for introducing and increasing your glory to the maximum in all the many strayed and indifferent souls*

All over the world we see unhappy, erring souls, who do not even know their purpose in life. They love all kinds of earthly goods instead of the one good, namely, God. Many, too, are indifferent to the highest love. We desire the "implanting and developing . . . in a most eminent degree" of the glory of the Immaculata in those souls. We beg her that we may be instruments in her immaculate and most loving hands, in order that she would not allow us to contradict her, that she constrain us, should we not want to listen to her.

*And thus help extend as far as possible the blessed kingdom of the most Sacred Heart of Jesus*

The most Sacred Heart of Jesus is the love of God toward men. His kingdom is the reign of love in the hearts of men, which Jesus manifested in the crib, throughout his life, on the cross and in the Eucharist, when he gave his mother as mother to us, and which (love) he desires to enkindle in human hearts. The implanting and developing of the honor of the Immaculata and the conquest of souls for her is the conquest of souls for Jesus' mother, who will carry the kingdom of Jesus into souls. For as far as possible,

*Wherever you enter, there you obtain the grace of conversion and growth in holiness, since it is through your hands that all graces come to us from the most Sacred Heart of Jesus*

The Immaculata is the "Omipotent Beseecher." Every conversion and sanctification is the work of grace, and she is the Mediatrix of All Graces. Hence she herself will suffice to beg and grant all and any graces. During the apparition of the Miraculous Medal, St. Catherine Laboure saw rays streaming from the rings on the fingers of the Immaculata. They represent graces that the Immaculata liberally bestows upon everyone who desires them. Alphonse Ratisbonne speaks similarly about the rays of grace in his vision.

*Allow me to praise you, O sacred Virgin.*
*Give me strength against your enemies.*

When Duns Scotus, a Franciscan, went to Paris for a dispute in which he was to defend the privi-

139

lege of the Immaculate Conception at the University of Sorbonne, he passed by a statue of the Blessed Mother and prayed to her with the above mentioned words. As tradition has it, the Blessed Mother bowed her head as a sign of confirmation.

In the first part of this petition Duns Scotus turns humbly to the Mother of God and asks that she permit him to praise her. Acknowledging his great unworthiness for such a sublime work as praising the Blessed Mother, he likewise acknowledges that grace depends upon her, and it is enough that she permit him, and his efforts will be crowned with success.

The second part is strong, unconditional, brave. As an instrument in her hand, he asks for strength to overcome the serpent.

Who is her enemy? Whatever is stained, whatever does not lead to God, whatever is not love, whatever comes from the hellish serpent, he himself is her enemy; hence it includes all our defects, or all our faults. We ask her to give us strength against him. For this one purpose all devotions exist, all prayers, the sacraments: that we receive power to overcome all obstacles in our striving for God in a more and more ardent love, in assimilating ourselves to God, in uniting with God himself. Just as we have come from God through a creature, so also we return to God. All nature tells us this. Wherever we glance, we see after action reaction, equal and opposite, and as it were, an echo of God's operation and his operation also in all creatures.

On the return road of reaction the being endowed with free will meets with difficulties and oppositions, and God permits these trials in order to strengthen that being so much the more in its striving towards him. In order that the being have sufficient strength for it, it must pray, it must ask for that strength from him, who is the source of all strength and who looks upon the efforts of his creature with love and desires that it come sincerely to him, for he does not stint his aid. Even if that creature, that dear child of his, stumbles on the way, falls, soils itself, wounds itself, that merciful Father cannot look upon its misfortune. He sends down his only begotten Son, who by his life and teaching points out to him a bright and sure road. By his Sacred Blood of infinite value he washes away the dirt and heals the wounds.

So that the soul from fear of the violated justice of God would not lose hope, God sends a personification of his love, the Spouse of the Spirit of motherly love, the Immaculata, all beautiful, without stain, though a daughter of men, sister of human beings. He commits the stewardship of his entire mercy towards souls. He constitutes her the Mediatrix of grace that was earned by her Son. He makes her the mother of grace, the mother of souls born of grace, reborn, and continually reborn in an always more perfect godlikeness.

*The above act of consecration and its explanation was written by St. Maximilian Kolbe, OFM CONV.*